Editing and Revising 7

Second Edition

by Sarah M. Williams and Dana Konopka

Edited by Patricia F. Braccio

Item Code QWK2035 • Copyright © 2011 Queue, Inc.

All rights reserved. No part of the material protected by this copyright may be reproduced or utilized in any form or by any means, electronic or mechanical, including photocopying, recording, or by any information storage and retrieval. Printed in the United States of America.

Queue, Inc., 703 Post Road, Fairfield, CT 06824
(800) 232-2224 • Fax: (800) 775-2729 • www.qworkbooks.com

TABLE OF CONTENTS

To the Students iv

1. The Twin Brothers 1
2. Should We Have a Longer School Day?....5
3. Ocean Microbes 8
4. What is a Democracy? 12
5. Raise Tax on Fast Food? 15
6. Henri Matisse 19
7. English's Jealousy 23
8. The Classical and Romantic Periods 27
9. I Deserve a Bigger Allowance 31
10. Lyme Disease 34
11. South Korea 38
12. The New SGA President 42
13. Spay and Neuter—Please! 46
14. John Calvin 50
15. Should We Send People to Mars? 54
16. A Hollow Earth 58
17. The New Neighbors 62
18. Poetic Peace..............................66
19. Some Hidden Jewels 70
20. From Paraguay 74
21. Greek Female Slaves 77
22. Two Respectable Men 81
23. Circadian Rhythm 85
24. Medgar Evers 89
25. The Best Sports Team Ever 92
26. Isolationism *vs.* Imperialism 96
27. Why Are Some People Allergic? 100
28. Origins of Astrology 104
29. Anger Management 108
30. Peer Tutoring 112
31. Film Critic 116
32. Advertisers Lure Teens 120
33. Snowboarding 124
34. Eating Disorders in Men? 127
35. Losing the Penan 131
36. Blogging 135
37. A Coral Feat 138
38. Is Stretching Unnecessary? 142
39. The Dwarf Gecko 145
40. New Coke 148
41. The Juggling Inmates 152
42. Jean-Jacques Rousseau 156
43. No More Censorship! 160
44. Tony Hawk 164
45. Bridges 168
46. Air Racing 172
47. An American Symbol 176
48. Magnetic Magic 180
49. Margaret Atwood 184
50. Chicago's Millennium Park 188
51. A Message from the Future 192
52. Delving into the Earth 196
53. Enhancing Reality 200
54. Thinking Ahead 204

TO THE STUDENTS

In this editing and revising workbook, you will read many passages. You will then answer multiple-choice questions about what you have read.

As you read and answer the questions, please remember:

- You may refer back to the passage as often as you like.
- Read each question very carefully and choose the **best** answer.
- Indicate the correct multiple-choice answers directly in this workbook. Circle or underline the correct answer.
- Remember what you know about correct grammar, punctuation, and English usage.

The Twin Brothers

Justin is in the seventh grade. His teacher asked each student to choose a myth that he or she liked and to summarize the story. Justin chose a Mexican myth. First, he made an outline of his ideas. Then he wrote his rough draft. Now he needs your help editing and revising it.

Here is Justin's rough draft. Read it and then answer questions 1–10.

1 The myth of the "Twin Brothers" is a famous Mexican myth that tells how the sun
2 and the moon came to be. It is the story of two brothers who were the grandsons of
3 the Father and Mother gods. The grandparents had helped Hurakan the god of
4 lightning, to create the earth.

5 Long ago there were two brother gods who were very good at playing a ball game
6 called "tlachtli." One day they make the mistake of playing very close to the edge of
7 Hades. The two kings that ruled Hades sent owl messengers to invite the two
8 brothers to a game of tlachtli. "Great! Now we can defeat our enemies," said the
9 brave brothers.

10 When the brothers got to Hades, they were killed. One of the brothers had fallen
11 in love with a princess of Hades and had secretly married her before his death. One
12 of the kings found out about this and drove her out of the kingdom. She came to the
13 earth and found the mother of her murdered husband. She bore twin sons and they
14 lived together with their grandmother and their two half-brothers.

15 The twin sons were named Hun-Apu and Xbalanque. Their half-brothers did not
16 like Hun-Apu and Xbalanque, the worst-behaved little boys in the world. When the
17 half-brothers teased the twins, Hun-Apu and Xbalanque turned them into something
18 else. When their grandmother gave them work to do in the fields and they didn't do
19 any of it. They cast a spell on the farm tools. The tools did all the work by themselves.

20 One day a rat told the twins the story about how their father and uncle had died
21 in Hades. The twins were determined to avenge their death. They went straight to
22 their grandmother and asked for the clubs and balls so they could go play tlachtli in
23 Hades. She gave them the clubs and balls, and off they went to Hades.

24 The rat had told Hun-Apu and Xbalanque about the tricks that the kings of Hades
25 had played on their father and uncle. The twins were ready for anything. They didn't
26 fall for any of the kings' tricks and they won the game of tlachtli. The kings got mad
27 and tried to kill them. Then they realized that Hun-Apu and Xbalanque were
28 immortal they could not be killed. The foolish kings tried to prove that they were
29 immortal, too. They said, "let us be killed, so that we can see what it's like to come
30 back to life, too." Then Hun-Apu and Xbalanque killed the kings, and they never
31 came back to life again.

32 The twins rescued the souls of their father and uncle and sent them into the
33 heavens. The father and uncle became the sun and the moon. They are still shining
34 in our skies today.

1. What is the **best** way to change the sentence in lines 3–4 (*The grandparents . . . the earth.*)?

    a. Change *lightning* to **lightening**.
    b. Insert a comma after **Hurakan**.
    c. Change *grandparents* to **Grandparents**.
    d. Make no change.

2. The sentence in lines 27–28 (*Then they . . . be killed.*) is poorly written. Which one of these is the **best** way to rewrite it?

    a. Then they realized that Hun-Apu and Xbalanque were immortal and could not be killed.
    b. Then they realized that Hun-Apu and Xbalanque because they were immortal they could not be killed.
    c. Then they, realizing that Hun-Apu and Xbalanque were immortal, could not be killed.
    d. Then they realized that Hun-Apu and Xbalanque were immortal could not be killed.

3. What is the **best** way to change the sentence in lines 29–30 (*They said . . . life, too."*)?

    a. Change *it's* to **its**.
    b. Delete the comma after **said**.
    c. Change *let* to **Let**.
    d. Make no change.

4. What is the **best** way to change the sentence in lines 6–7 (*One day . . . of Hades.*)?

    a. Change *to* to **too**.
    b. Change *Hades* to **hades**.
    c. Change *make* to **made**.
    d. Make no change.

5. Where is there an incomplete sentence?

    a. in lines 7–8 (*The two . . . of tlachtli.*)
    b. in lines 18–19 (*When their . . . of it.*)
    c. in lines 28–29 (*The foolish . . . immortal, too.*)
    d. in lines 32–33 (*The twins . . . the heavens.*)

6. Which of the following is the **best** way to combine the two sentences in line 19 (*They cast . . . by themselves.*)?

   a. Doing all the work by themselves, they cast a spell on the farm tools.
   b. They cast a spell on the farm tools the tools did all the work by themselves.
   c. They cast a spell on the farm tools and who did all the work by themselves.
   d. They cast a spell on the farm tools, and the tools did all the work by themselves.

7. Which of the following would be the **best** way to rewrite the sentence in lines 16–18 (*When the . . . something else.*) to make it more specific?

   a. When the half-brothers teased the twins, Hun-Apu and Xbalanque turned them into different animals.
   b. When the half-brothers teased the twins, Hun-Apu and Xbalanque turned them to be different from what they were before.
   c. When the half-brothers teased the twins, Hun-Apu and Xbalanque turned them into a couple of silly-looking apes.
   d. When the half-brothers teased the twins, Hun-Apu and Xbalanque turned them to make them look silly.

8. Justin wants to add the following sentence to the fifth paragraph: *The grandmother was reluctant, but she knew the boys had a job to do.* The sentence would **best** fit

   a. after the sentence in lines 20–21 (*One day . . . in Hades.*).
   b. after the sentence in line 21 (*The twins . . . their death.*).
   c. after the sentence in lines 21–23 (*They went . . . in Hades.*).
   d. after the sentence in line 23 (*She gave . . . to Hades.*).

9. What is the **best** way to change the sentence in lines 25–26 (*They didn't . . . of tlachtli.*)?

   a. Change *kings'* to **king's**.
   b. Change *fall* to **fell**.
   c. Change the *period* to a **question mark**.
   d. Make no change.

10. Which transition would **best** fit at the beginning of the sentence in lines 15–16 (*Their half-brothers . . . the world.*)?
    a. First,
    b. Unfortunately,
    c. For example,
    d. Moreover,

Should We Have a Longer School Day?

Kenita is in the seventh grade. The Board of Education is considering making the school day longer by one hour each day. Kenita's teacher asked each student to write a letter to the school superintendent to persuade her to accept or reject this idea. Kenita organized her ideas and wrote her rough draft. Now she needs your help editing and revising it.

Here is Kenita's rough draft. Read it and then answer questions 1–10.

1   dear Dr. Frenette,

2   I know that you have reasons for wanting to make the school day one hour longer.
3   A longer school day would allow students more time to learn. Teachers would have
4   more time to help students who need extra help. Students could do enrichment
5   projects who were done with their work. A longer school day would help working
6   parents because their children will be safe at school in the afternoon.

7   I still think that making the school day one hour longer is not the best idea.
8   Us kids are not like grownups who can work a long day. By three o'clock in the
9   afternoon, most kids are already pretty tired from all that school work. Before
10 tackling our homework we need to go rest our brains.

11   When I need extra help with my work, I bring it to Mrs. Pow, and she always helps
12 me figure it out. Sometimes I learn from my classmates, too. However, I learn best
13 when I focus on the task and work by myself. I can do that at home or in the after-
14 school program, and I don't need an extra hour of classes to learn more. Sometimes
15 I think it's better we having to do things by ourselves. It makes us more independent.

16   If you are worried about the safety of students who's parents work, I think you
17 should make the after-school program available to everyone for free. Then the
18 students would be safe and the parents would have peace of mind the kids would be
19 able to play or get their homework done. I like the relaxed atmosphere in the after-
20 school program. Maybe there could be special classes once in a while that the
21 students could choose to take. I would like to learn photography.

22   I hope that you will agree that improving the after-school program would be
23 better than making the school day one hour longer. Thank you for considering my
24 opinion.

25   Sincerely,

26   Kenita Williams

1. What is the **best** way to change the sentence in line 8 (*Us kids . . . long day.*)?
   a. Change *Us* to **We**.
   b. Insert a comma after **grownups**.
   c. Change *are* to **is**.
   d. Make no change.

2. What is the **best** way to change the sentence in lines 9–10 (*Before tackling . . . our brains.*)?
   a. Change *brains* to **brians**.
   b. Change *our* to **hour**.
   c. Insert a comma after **homework**.
   d. Make no change.

3. What is the **best** way to change the sentence in lines 16–17 (*If you . . . for free.*)?
   a. Change *you should* to **me should**.
   b. Change *who's* to **whose**.
   c. Change *available* to **availlable**.
   d. Make no change.

4. The sentence in lines 17–19 (*Then the . . . homework done.*) is poorly written. Which one of these is the **best** way to rewrite it?
   a. Then the students would be safe, the parents would have peace of mind, and the kids would be able to play or get their homework done.
   b. Then the students would be safe and the parents would have peace of mind and the kids would be able to play or get their homework done.
   c. Then the students would be safe. And the parents would have peace of mind and the kids would be able to play or get their homework done.
   d. Then the students would be safe. The parents would have peace of mind. The kids would be able to play. Or they could get their homework done.

5. The topic sentence of the first paragraph is in
   a. line 3 (*A longer . . . to learn.*).
   b. lines 3–4 (*Teachers would . . . extra help.*).
   c. lines 4–5 (*Students could . . . their work.*).
   d. lines 5–6 (*A longer . . . the afternoon.*).

6. How should Kenita edit the opening (line 1)?

   a. Change *Dr.* to **dr.**
   b. Change the *comma* to a **question mark**.
   c. Change *dear* to **Dear**.
   d. Make no change.

7. What is the **best** way to change the sentence in line 12 (*Sometimes I . . . classmates, too.*)?

   a. Change *too* to **two**.
   b. Insert a comma after **learn**.
   c. Change *my* to **his**.
   d. Make no change.

8. The sentence in lines 4–5 (*Students could . . . their work.*) is poorly written. Which one of these is the **best** way to rewrite it?

   a. Students could do enrichment projects that were done with their work.
   b. Students who were done with their work could do enrichment projects.
   c. Students could do enrichment projects being done with their work.
   d. Who were done with their work, students could do enrichment projects.

9. The sentence in lines 14–15 (*Sometimes I . . . by ourselves.*) is poorly written. Which one of these is the **best** way to rewrite it?

   a. Sometimes I think having better things to do by ourselves.
   b. Sometimes I think it's better we are, to do things by ourselves.
   c. Sometimes I think it's better we were having to do things by ourselves.
   d. Sometimes I think it's better when we have to do things by ourselves.

10. What is the **best** way to change the sentence in lines 5–6 (*A longer . . . the afternoon.*)?

    a. Change *will* to **would**.
    b. Change *their* to **they're**.
    c. Insert a comma after **parents**.
    d. Make no change.

OCEAN MICROBES 3

Brian's seventh-grade teacher asked each student to write a report about ocean microbes and the role that they play in our world. Brian took notes at the library, organized his thoughts, and wrote his rough draft. Now he needs your help editing and revising it.

Here is Brian's rough draft. Read it and then answer questions 1–10.

1   Every drop of ocean water is alive with tiny sea creatures called "microbes." A
2   microbe is a living organism that is too small to be seen without a microscope. Most
3   of these microbes are one-celled organisms called "bacteria." Maybe these little
4   creatures don't seem very significant, but they are if it weren't for them, life as we
5   know it could not exist.

6   Ocean bacteria are the most commonest creatures on the planet. There are
7   billions of them in just one teaspoon of sea water. Even though the microbes are so
8   tiny, scientists believe that if we put them all together, they would weigh as much as
9   all the fish in the oceans combind.

10 Ocean bacteria has some very important jobs to do. Some bacteria live close to the
11 surface where they get a lot of sunlight. These bacteria carry out photosynthesis.
12 They produce about one-half of all the oxygen that we breathe. Some bacteria live in
13 the deeper waters instead. It's hard to believe that there could be life in such a deep,
14 dark place. These cool bacteria have evolved to get their energy from chemicals
15 instead of the sun. They are responsible for decomposing dead material that falls to
16 the bottom of the ocean. Ocean bacteria affect the amount of carbon that is present
17 in the ocean. Carbon is an element that is necessary for all living things. The
18 amount of carbon in the ocean affects how much carbon dioxide there is in the earth's
19 atmosphere.

20 Living in the deepest ocean rocks, scientists recently discovered bacteria. They
21 eat chemicals and can live without any light in almost boiling hot water. They get
22 their energy from the minerals in the rocks. Some scientists believe that these
23 bacteria could exist beneath the surface of Mars.

24 Imagine the world without ocean bacteria. The sea would be full of dead
25 creatures, and the land creatures would not have enough oxygen to breathe. There
26 might been enough carbon dioxide in our atmosphere to raise temperatures all over
27 the world. Ocean microbes are a extremely important part of life on Earth.

1. What is the **best** way to change the sentence in lines 25–27 (*There might . . . the world.*)?

   a. Change *to* to **too**.
   b. Insert a comma after **dioxide**.
   c. Change *been* to **be**.
   d. Make no change.

2. The sentence in lines 3–5 (*Maybe these . . . not exist.*) is poorly written. Which one of these is the **best** way to rewrite it?

   a. Maybe these little creatures don't seem very significant, but they are, and if it weren't for them, life as we know it, could not exist.
   b. Maybe these little creatures don't seem very significant, but they are. If it weren't for them, life as we know it could not exist.
   c. Maybe these little creatures don't seem very significant. But they are if it weren't for them, life as we know it could not exist.
   d. Maybe these little creatures don't seem very significant. But they are if it weren't for them. Life as we know it could not exist.

3. What is the **best** way to change the sentence in lines 7–9 (*Even though . . . oceans combind.*)?

   a. Change *combind* to **combined**.
   b. Change *all together* to **altogether**.
   c. Change *are* to **is**.
   d. Make no change.

4. What is the **best** way to change the sentence in line 10 (*Ocean bacteria . . . to do.*)?

   a. Change *bacteria* to **bacterias**.
   b. Change *has* to **have**.
   c. Change *to* to **two**.
   d. Make no change.

5. Which of the following is the **best** supporting detail to add after the sentence in lines 17–19 (*The amount . . . earth's atmosphere.*)?

   a. Ocean microbes are some of the tiniest known living things.
   b. Can you imagine what would happen if there were an underwater earthquake?
   c. Earth's atmosphere is denser than that of Mars.
   d. Carbon dioxide is a gas that contributes to global warming.

6. Which transition would **best** fit at the beginning of the sentence in lines 14–15 (*These cool . . . the sun.*)?

   a. However,
   b. Unfortunately,
   c. In addition,
   d. Moreover,

7. What is the **best** way to change the sentence in line 6 (*Ocean bacteria . . . the planet.*)?

   a. Change *bacteria* to **bacterias**.
   b. Change *commonest* to **common**.
   c. Change *are* to **is**.
   d. Make no change.

8. Which of the following would be the **best** way to rewrite the sentence in lines 14–15 (*These cool . . . the sun.*) to make it more specific?

   a. These neat bacteria have evolved to get their energy from chemicals instead of the sun.
   b. These good bacteria have evolved to get their energy from chemicals instead of the sun.
   c. These hardy bacteria have evolved to get their energy from chemicals instead of the sun.
   d. These interesting bacteria have evolved to get their energy from chemicals instead of the sun.

9. The sentence in line 20 (*Living in . . . discovered bacteria.*) is poorly written. Which one of these is the **best** way to rewrite it?

   a. Living in the deepest ocean rocks that the scientists recently discovered bacteria.
   b. Scientists, living in the deepest ocean rocks, recently discovered bacteria.
   c. Scientists recently discovered bacteria living in the deepest ocean rocks.
   d. In the deepest ocean rocks living, scientists recently discovered bacteria.

10. What is the **best** way to change the sentence in line 27 (*Ocean microbes . . . on Earth.*)?

   a. Change *a* to **an**.
   b. Change *Earth* to **earth**.
   c. Insert a comma after **extremely**.
   d. Make no change.

What Is a Democracy?

Shelby's seventh-grade class is learning about different forms of government. Her teacher asked each student to reflect on all that the class had learned and to write an essay describing his or her own personal definition of a democracy. Shelby made an outline of her ideas and then wrote her rough draft. Now she needs your help editing and revising it.

Here is Shelby's rough draft. Read it and then answer questions 1–10.

1 What is a democracy? This is a very tough question. I think that each person
2 would have a slightly different definition of a democracy.

3 To me, the word, "democracy," means "fairness." A democracy is a system of
4 government that tries to be fair to each and every person. In a democracy, there's no
5 dictators and no ruling classes. In a democracy, the people vote to elect their leaders,
6 and the leaders serve the people. In a democracy, everyone can participate in the
7 government. There is no discrimination against anyone because of his or her race,
8 gender, or religion. People are free to speak their minds against the government
9 without having to be afraid of punishment. In a democracy, people can live the way
10 they want to live without the government telling them where they have to live, what
11 they have to wear, or what they have to believe.

12 In a democracy, everyone should be able to live the way he or she wants to live.
13 However, it's not as simple as it sounds. Suppose you are a scientist and you want to
14 experiment with some deadly viruses in your home laboratory. Then the government
15 finds out what you are doing. The government forces you to give up your research.
16 You might say "That's not fair!" It isn't fair to your community, though, when you put
17 people's lives in jeopardy. In a democracy, an individual's rights are honored only as
18 long as they are not a threat other people. To be fair, a democracy has to have some
19 limits.

20 Governments are not the only things that can be called democracies. A dictator is
21 a person who has absolute power over the people in his or her country. A home could
22 be a democracy. If all the members of a family work together to make the house
23 rules, then their home is a democracy.

24 People who live in a democracy have some important responsibilities. It isn't any
25 good to live in a democracy and then not vote, not learn what's going on, and not
26 speak up for what we believe. Then nothing will ever change for the better. We
27 americans are fortunate to live in a democratic society. Paying attention to our
28 country and making it an even better place someday.

1. The topic sentence of the third paragraph is in the sentence in
   a. line 12 (*In a . . . to live.*).
   b. line 15 (*The government . . . your research.*).
   c. lines 16–17 (*It isn't . . . in jeopardy.*).
   d. lines 18–19 (*To be . . . some limits.*).

2. What is the **best** way to change the sentence in line 16 (*You might . . . not fair!*)?
   a. Insert a comma after **say**.
   b. Change the *exclamation point* to a **question mark**.
   c. Change *That's* to **Thats**.
   d. Make no change.

3. What is the **best** way to rewrite the sentence in lines 6–7 (*In a . . . the government.*) to improve the paragraph?
   a. In a democracy, it's where everyone can participate in the government.
   b. Everyone can participate in a democratic government.
   c. In a democracy, everyone in the government can participate.
   d. Everyone in a democracy can participate in the government.

4. Which of the following is the **best** supporting to detail to add after the sentence in lines 22–23 (*If all . . . a democracy.*)?
   a. The president is the elected leader of our country.
   b. I am glad that the United States is a democratic country.
   c. India is called "the largest democracy in the world," but its government is very different from our government.
   d. At school, our classroom is a democracy when we take votes.

5. Which one of these sentences does **not** belong?
   a. the sentence in lines 3–4 (*A democracy . . . every person.*)
   b. the sentence in lines 9–11 (*In a . . . to believe.*)
   c. the sentence in line 16 (*You might . . . not fair!*)
   d. the sentence in lines 20–21 (*A dictator . . . her country.*)

6. What is the **best** way to change the sentence in lines 26–27 (*We americans . . . democratic society.*)?

   a. Change *are* to **is**.
   b. Change *americans* to **Americans**.
   c. Change *a* to **an**.
   d. Make no change.

7. Which of the following is the **best** way to combine the two sentences in lines 14–15 (*Then the . . . your research.*)?

   a. Then the government finds out what you are doing because the government forces you to give up your research.
   b. Then the government finds out what you are doing, the government forces you to give up your research.
   c. Then the government finds out what you are doing and forces you to give up your research.
   d. Then the government finds out what you are doing but it forces you to give up your research.

8. Where is there an incomplete sentence?

   a. in lines 9–11 (*In a . . . to believe.*)
   b. in lines 13–14 (*Suppose you . . . home laboratory.*)
   c. in lines 22–23 (*If all . . . a democracy.*)
   d. in lines 27–28 (*Paying attention . . . place someday.*)

9. What is the **best** way to change the sentence in lines 4–5 (*In a . . . ruling classes.*)?

   a. Change *ruling* to **rooling**.
   b. Change *There's* to **There are**.
   c. Insert a comma after **dictators**.
   d. Make no change.

10. What is the **best** way to change the sentence in lines 22–23 (*If all . . . a democracy.*)?

    a. Change *then* to **than**.
    b. Change *home* to **homes**.
    c. Change *their* to **they're**.
    d. Make no change.

Raise Tax on Fast Food?

Joel is in the seventh grade. His teacher asked each student to think about what would happen if the taxes were raised on fast food. Each student then had to decide whether or not he or she supported the tax hike and to explain why or why not. Joel organized his thoughts and wrote the rough draft of a persuasive essay. Now he needs your help editing and revising it.

Here is Joel's rough draft. Read it and then answer questions 1–10.

1   Everybody knows that eating too much fast food is bad for your health. Some
2 people think that if we raised the taxes on fast food, people would eat less of it and
3 be healthier. Sure, we could use the extra tax money to spend on education or health
4 care. I do not agree that raising taxes on fast food is a good idea.

5   I think that raising taxes on fast food is unfair to the restaurants. This is a
6 country of equal oportunity, and it doesn't seem right to me that the government
7 would make it harder for certain restaurants to sell their food. It isn't like the
8 restaurants are selling cigarettes. Cigarettes have been proven to cause cancer. Fast
9 food may be bad for you, but most people do not eat them every day. In addition, most
10 fast food restaurants today also sell some healthy food. How would we ever decide
11 which foods get taxed and which ones didn't? I would not like to be the store manager
12 who has to keep track of all the different tax rates for the items on the menu.

13   Raising taxes are also unfair to the customers. What we eat is a personal choice.
14 I think it would be unfair for the government to charge extra tax for certain foods that
15 people choose to eat. Then it would no longer be a truly free choice. When you go
16 into a fast food restaurant you always see families with kids eating there. They want
17 a quick and easy meal that everyone likes, and they don't want to pay a lot for it.
18 A tax on fast food, more difficult for families to eat out.

19   There is another problem with taxing fast food. Restaurants are not the only
20 place where we can buy fast food. Grocery stores sell it, too. Who decides which
21 grocery store items get taxed and which ones don't? We would need a federal bureau
22 with fast food patrol units all over the country. My father is a police officer. It doesn't
23 seem very practical to me.

24   Fast food is not the healthiest kind of food in the world, but it does not deserve
25 the punishment of added taxes. There are better ways to raise money for health and
26 education. Let's get real and tax all food equally.

1. The sentence in lines 15–16 (*When you . . . eating there.*) is poorly written. Which one of these is the **best** way to rewrite it?

    a. When you go into a fast food restaurant. You always see families with kids eating there.
    b. When you go into a fast food restaurant, you always see families with kids eating there.
    c. When you go into a fast food restaurant and always see families with kids eating there.
    d. When you go into a fast food restaurant, you always see, families with kids eating there.

2. Which one of these transitions would **best** fit at the beginning of the sentence in line 4 (*I do . . . good idea.*)?

    a. For example,
    b. In addition,
    c. However,
    d. Fortunately,

3. What is the **best** way to change the sentence in line 13 (*Raising taxes . . . the customers.*)?

    a. Change *to* to **too**.
    b. Change *customers* to **customer**.
    c. Change *are* to **is**.
    d. Make no change.

4. Where is there an incomplete sentence?

    a. line 5 (*I think . . . the restaurants.*)
    b. lines 8–9 (*Fast food . . . every day.*)
    c. line 18 (*A tax . . . eat out.*)
    d. lines 22–23 (*It doesn't . . . to me.*)

5. Which of the following is the **best** way to combine the two sentences in lines 7–8 (*It isn't . . . cause cancer.*)?

    a. It isn't like the restaurants are selling cigarettes have been proven to cause cancer.
    b. It isn't like the restaurants are selling cigarettes but cigarettes have been proven to cause cancer.
    c. Proven to cause cancer, the restaurants are not selling cigarettes.
    d. It isn't like the restaurants are selling cigarettes, which have been proven to cause cancer.

6. What is the **best** way to change the sentence in lines 8–9 (*Fast food . . . every day.*)?

    a. Change *them* to **it**.
    b. Change *most* to **mostest**.
    c. Change *do* to **does**.
    d. Make no change.

7. What is the **best** way to change the sentence in lines 10–11 (*How would . . . ones didn't?*)?

    a. Change the *question mark* to an **exclamation point**.
    b. Change *taxed* to **taxxed**.
    c. Change *didn't* to **don't**.
    d. Make no change.

8. Which one of these sentences does **not** belong?

    a. the sentence in lines 3–4 (*Sure, we . . . health care.*)
    b. the sentence in lines 5–7 (*This is . . . their food.*)
    c. the sentence in line 13 (*What we . . . personal choice.*)
    d. the sentence in line 22 (*My father . . . police officer.*)

9. Instead of the sentence in line 26 (*Let's get . . . food equally.*), which one of these uses the **best** tone for this audience?

    a. Let's get a grip and tax all food equally.
    b. Come on, let's just tax all food equally.
    c. Let's be fair and tax all food equally.
    d. Don't be ridiculous. Let's tax all fast food equally.

10. What is the **best** way to change the sentence in lines 5–7 (*This is . . . their food.*)?
    a. Change *oportunity* to **opportunity**.
    b. Change *their* to **they're**.
    c. Change *doesn't* to **don't**.
    d. Make no change.

HENRI MATISSE

Heidi's seventh-grade French class has been studying French painters and sculptors. Her teacher requests that each student write a report on an artist of his or her choosing. Heidi loves Henri Matisse's work and decides to write her report about him. After researching and writing her first draft, she needs some help revising it.

Here is Heidi's rough draft. Read it and then answer questions 1–10.

1 Henri Matisse was one of the most famous French artists of all time. He was an
2 accomplished sculptor, painter, and graphic designer. As leader of a movement called
3 "Fauvism," Matisse left a bold mark on art as we know it today.

4 Henri Matisse was born on December 31, 1869, in Le Cateau in France. He have
5 been described as a slow, methodical leader who taught and encouraged other
6 painters. Some biographers say he was an anxious man, who eased his nervousness
7 by painting. Matisse himself described his art as "a good armchair." Another way of
8 saying that it was a comfort to him.

9 Matisse first began painting while recovering from an operation. He moved to
10 Paris in 1891 to study art. Less than a decade after moving to Paris, Matisse was
11 leading a group of artists called the "Fauvists." Fauvism flourished in France from
12 1898 to 1908. These artists used pure, brilliant color—often straight from the tube—
13 to create what has been described as "an explosion on the canvas." Matisse believed
14 that the arrangement of color in a piece of art was as important in communicating
15 meaning as the painting's subject matter. He chose to paint bright colors and strong
16 lines over detail, a style that greatly differed from the Impressionist painters of the
17 late nineteenth and early twentieth centuries. Fauvists did like the Impressionists
18 did and painted directly from nature, but the works they did were more expressive
19 and less traditional.

20 In 1905, Matisse and other Fauvists exhibited their paintings at the Salon
21 d'Automne for the first time. The bright colors and bold forms shocked the Paris art
22 world. Matisse exbihited his famous *Woman with the Hat*. This painting has brisk
23 strokes of blue, green, and red. The colors and strokes form an energetic, expressive
24 view of a woman. A critic of the time Louis Vauxcelles called the painters "Les
25 Fauves," which translates to "Wild Beasts." He found their work to be too violent.

26 In 1941, following a rich artistic career, Matisse was diagnosed with duodenal
27 cancer. He was confined to a wheelchair. But he didn't stop working anyway. When
28 he was too weak to stand at his easel, he began papercuts, or colored-paper collages.
29 The 1950 piece *Beasts of the Sea* gives you the feeling that you are underwater among
30 fish, sea horses, and coral.

31 Henri Matisse died on November 3, 1954, in Nice in France. His artistic path was
32 long and varied, covering many different styles along the way. Overall, we see that
33 he was one of the finest, most influential artists of our time.

1. What is the **best** way to rewrite the sentence in lines 10–11 (*Less than . . . the "Fauvists."*) to improve the paragraph?

    a. Less than a decade after Matisse was leading a group of artists called "Fauvists," he had already moved to Paris.
    b. Less than a decade later, Matisse was leading a group of artists called "Fauvists."
    c. A group of artists called "Fauvists" led Matisse less than a decade after he moved to Paris.
    d. A decade after Matisse moved to Paris, the "Fauvists" were being led by Matisse.

2. Where is there an incomplete sentence?

    a. in lines 17–19 (*Fauvists painted . . . less traditional.*)
    b. in line 25 (*He found . . . too violent.*)
    c. in lines 7–8 (*Another way . . . to him.*)
    d. in line 31 (*Henri Matisse . . . in France.*)

3. What is the **best** change, if any, to make in the sentence in lines 24–25 (*A critic . . . "Wild Beasts."*)?

    a. Insert commas before and after **Louis Vauxcelles**.
    b. Change *painters* to **Painters**.
    c. Insert a comma after **to**.
    d. Make no change.

4. What is the **best** change, if any, to make in the sentence in line 22 (*Matisse exbihited . . . the Hat.*)?

    a. Change *famous* to **famus**.
    b. Change *exbihited* to **exhibited**.
    c. Change the *period* to an **exclamation point**.
    d. Make no change.

5. Instead of the sentence in line 27 (*But he . . . working anyway.*), which one of these sentences uses the **best** tone for this audience?

    a. Still, he continued working as an artist.
    b. Nothing could stop him cuz he just wanted to work.
    c. Working as an artist was real special to him.
    d. He could keep working because he wanted to.

6. Which of the following is the **best** way to combine the two sentences in lines 22–24 (*This painting . . . a woman.*)?

   a. This painting of an energetic, expressive woman is done in brisk strokes of blue, green, and red.
   b. Blue, green, and red form an energetic, expressive view of a woman in the painting.
   c. This painting forms an energetic, expressive woman's view of blue, green, and red.
   d. This painting has brisk strokes of blue, green, and red that form an energetic, expressive view of a woman.

7. The topic sentence in the fourth paragraph is in the sentence in

   a. lines 24–25 (*A critic . . . "Wild Beasts."*).
   b. lines 22–23 (*This painting . . . and red.*).
   c. lines 20–21 (*In 1905 . . . first time.*).
   d. line 25 (*He found . . . too violent.*).

8. What is the **best** change, if any, to make in the sentence in lines 31–32 (*His artistic . . . the way.*)?

   a. Insert a comma after **long**.
   b. Change *varied* to **vareed**.
   c. Change *was* to **were**.
   d. Make no change.

9. What is the **best** change, if any, to make in the sentence in lines 4–6 (*He have . . . other painters.*)?

   a. Change *methodical* to **methodicical**.
   b. Change *have* to **has**.
   c. Change the *comma* to a **period**.
   d. Make no change.

10. The sentence in lines 17–19 (*Fauvists did . . . less traditional.*) is poorly written. Which one of these is the **best** way to rewrite it?

    a. Fauvists painted directly from nature as the Impressionists had before them, but their works were more expressive and less traditional.
    b. Impressionists painted directly from nature and so did the Fauvists, and their works were more expressive and less traditional.
    c. Fauvists and Impressionists both painted from nature, but the Fauvists did works that were more expressive and they did works that were less traditional.
    d. Impressionists and Fauvists, directly from nature they painted, but their works were more expressive and less traditional.

English's Jealousy

Drew has been learning about dialogue and creative writing in his seventh-grade English class. The teacher told the students that they must write a creative story with dialogue. Drew brainstormed some ideas and made a web of elements he wanted to include. He wrote his first draft and needs help editing and revising part of it.

Here is Drew's rough draft. Read it and then answer questions 1–10.

1 "I can't take it!" The man clenched his meaty hands against his temples and
2 locked his jaw. "The stress will kill me, I swear it!" His massive shoulders seemed
3 to swell out from under a undersized overcoat, a relic of a time when men wore suits
4 no matter what their employ. "Could it be that I don't write as good as I think I do?"

5 "Impossible, Evan," replied a frail man who seemed made of the most thinner
6 crepe. His iridescent skin revealed his slight bone structure. His hollowed eyes hung
7 loosely in they're sockets, and his cheekbones were sharp points jutting out from a
8 concave face. "This is what you were destined to become. You were meant to be the
9 world's most famous author and you will be! I bet my life on it."

10 Evan Driscoll drove his pen into the tabletop. "I've had enough of your groveling,"
11 he snarled. "You will be a world-famous editor the moment I become a world-famous
12 author and no sooner. You'll get no scraps from me by trying to lick my boot heels like
13 a common peasant."

14 Driscoll's monstrous frame shuddered and heaved as he tried to summon the
15 strength to continue. His assistant, the sniveling Mr. Edwin McGrue, hovered in his
16 shadow, taking the completed pages of Driscoll's scrawling handwriting from him and
17 laying them aside in a wooden box. Night after night, long after Driscoll had retired
18 for rest, McGrue methodically tossed each page into a roaring fire in his employer's own
19 living room. In time, the madness would pass and Driscoll would became aware of
20 Edwin's deceit. However, by that time, McGrue would be back with the man who hired
21 him for such a task: Samuel English, creative writer and dialogue magician.

22 Unfortunately, English's longstanding talent had waned in the past few years and
23 his greatest competition, Evan Driscoll was slated to become the world's most
24 acclaimed author of our time. English's novels had graced the bookstands of stores
25 across the country, but Driscoll was steadily conquering the world. It became
26 Englishs' only desire—far beyond becoming a fine writer—to demolish Driscoll's
27 career.

28 It was Edwin McGrue's task to pour tinctures into Driscoll's coffee as he worked.
29 These potions would still his thinking processes and drive him to the point of
30 madness, which they were designed to. English had come upon these tinctures from
31 a secretive source hidden in the back allies of Marysport. McGrue remorselessly
32 polluted Driscoll's coffee with these flavorless concoctions.

1. Which of the following is the **best** closing sentence for the last paragraph?

    a. McGrue lived in a small apartment.
    b. Driscoll had yet to discover the horrifying truth.
    c. English and Driscoll met in a train station just outside of Marysport.
    d. Frankly, writing was McGrue's most loathsome task.

2. What is the **best** change, if any, to make in the sentence in line 4 (*"Could it . . . I do?"*)?

    a. Change the *question mark* to a **period**.
    b. Change *good* to **well**.
    c. Insert a comma after **be**.
    d. Make no change.

3. What is the **best** change, if any, to make in the sentence in lines 25–27 (*It became . . . Driscoll's career.*)?

    a. Change *Englishs'* to **English's**.
    b. Change *demolish* to **deemolish**.
    c. Change *writer* to **writer**.
    d. Make no change.

4. The sentence in lines 29–30 (*These potions . . . designed to.*) is poorly written. Which one of these is the **best** way to rewrite it?

    a. His thinking processes having been stilled and his madness having been driven, these potions worked as they were designed to.
    b. By driving him to the point of madness, these potions were designed to still his thinking processes.
    c. These potions were designed to still his thinking processes and drive him to the point of madness.
    d. These potions were designed, and stilled his thinking process and drove him to the point of madness.

5. Drew wants to add the following sentence to the last paragraph: *Their origin had even been concealed from his shifty companion.* The sentence would **best** fit

   a. after the sentence in line 28 (*It was . . . he worked.*).
   b. after the sentence in lines 29–30 (*These potions . . . designed to.*).
   c. after the sentence in lines 30–31 (*English had . . . of Marysport.*).
   d. after the sentence in lines 31–32 (*McGrue remorselessly . . . flavorless concoctions.*).

6. What is the **best** change, if any, to make in the sentence in lines 2–4 (*His massive . . . their employ.*)?

   a. Change *a* to **an**.
   b. Change *swell* to **swelled**.
   c. Insert a comma after **out**.
   d. Make no change.

7. What is the **best** change, if any, to make in the sentence in lines 6–8 (*His hollowed . . . concave face.*)?

   a. Change *hung* to **hang**.
   b. Change *they're* to **their**.
   c. Change *loosely* to **losely**.
   d. Make no change.

8. What is the **best** change, if any, to make in the sentence in lines 22–24 (*Unfortunately, English's . . . our time.*)?

   a. Change the *period* to a **question mark**.
   b. Change *our* to **hour**.
   c. Insert a comma after **Evan Driscoll**.
   d. Make no change.

9. What is the **best** change, if any, to make in the sentence in lines 30–31 (*English had . . . of Marysport.*)?

   a. Change *tinctures* to **tincture**.
   b. Change *allies* to **alleys**.
   c. Insert a comma after **hidden**.
   d. Make no change.

10. What is the **best** change, if any, to make in the sentence in lines 5–6 (*"Impossible, Evan . . . thinner crepe.*)?

    a. Change *crepe* to **Crepe**.
    b. Change *Evan,"* to **Evan."**
    c. Change *most thinner* to **thinnest**.
    d. Make no change.

The Classical and Romantic Periods

Julia is in the seventh grade. Her music class is studying classical music, and her teacher asked each student to write a short paper comparing and contrasting the classical and romantic periods in music. Julia took notes from her library books, made an outline, and then wrote her rough draft. Now she needs your help editing and revising it.

Here is Julia's rough draft. Read it and then answer questions 1–10.

1 Many people think that all music that is not popular music, rock music, or jazz is
2 "classical" music. I used to think so, too. Now I know that what I used to call
3 "classical" music might be either Baroque, Classical, Romantic, or Modern music.
4 Let's take a look at the Classical and Romantic periods in music.

5 The Classical period lasted from about 1720 to about 1800. The "Enlightenment"
6 was going on in europe at this time. The Enlightenment was a way of thinking about
7 life. People started to believe that the individual person was more important then
8 the government or society. They believed that the answers to all questions could be
9 found in nature, and they believed that knowledge and reason could solve any
10 problem. People valued balance, order, and logic during the Enlightenment.

11 The Enlightenment influenced music during the Classical period. Composers
12 started trying to write music that was very structured and balanced without being
13 too emotional. People during the Enlightenment believed that all human beings were
14 under the same universal, natural law. Composers in several countries tried to follow
15 the same rules for writing music. Franz Joseph Haydn, Wolfgang Amadeus Mozart
16 and Ludwig van Beethoven were Classical composers.

17 The Romantic period lasted from about 1800 up to World War I. Freedom,
18 movement, and emotion were the most important things to Romantic composers.
19 Composers stopped trying to follow the same rules as everyone else. They started
20 expressing their own emotions in their music they stopped trying so hard to please
21 their "patrons." A patron was a very wealthy person who supported a musician
22 paying money.

23 During the Romantic period, the middle class became more able to pay for
24 concerts and music lessons. Romantic composers played for large audienses, not just
25 small groups of wealthy patrons. Some of them became as popular as pop stars are
26 to us today. Some Romantic composers were Franz Shubert, Robert Schumann,
27 Johannes Brahms, and Peter Tchaikovsky.

28 Romantic composers wanted to express their individual creativity, but they did
29 not totally abandon Classical techniques. The music changed quite a bit, but much
30 more radical changes would come later in the twentieth century.

1. The topic sentence of the third paragraph is in the sentence in
    a. line 11 (*The Enlightenment . . . Classical period.*).
    b. lines 11–13 (*Composers started . . . too emotional.*).
    c. lines 14–15 (*Composers in . . . writing music.*).
    d. lines 15–16 (*Franz Joseph . . . Classical composers.*).

2. Which of the following is the **best** supporting detail to add after the sentence in lines 8–10 (*They believed . . . any problem.*)?
    a. The Romantic period lasted longer than the Classical period.
    b. People became very interested in science.
    c. The Modern movement started around the time of World War I.
    d. Most of the middle class did not have the means to pay for music lessons.

3. What is the **best** change, if any, to make in the sentence in lines 15–16 (*Franz Joseph . . . Classical composers.*)?
    a. Change *Classical* to **classical**.
    b. Insert a comma after **Mozart**.
    c. Change *van* to **Van**.
    d. Make no change.

4. What is the **best** change, if any, to make in the sentence in lines 23–24 (*During the . . . music lessons.*)?
    a. Change *Romantic* to **romantic**.
    b. Insert a comma after **class**.
    c. Insert a comma after **During**.
    d. Make no change.

5. What is the **best** change, if any, to make in the sentence in lines 5–6 (*The "Enlightenment" . . . this time.*)?
    a. Change *"Enlightenment"* to **"Enlightenment,"**.
    b. Change *"Enlightenment"* to **"enlightenment"**.
    c. Change *europe* to **Europe**.
    d. Make no change.

6. The sentence in lines 19–21 (*They started . . . their "patrons."*) is poorly written. Which one of these is the **best** way to rewrite it?

   a. They started expressing their own emotions in their music trying so hard to please their "patrons."
   b. They stopped trying so hard to please their "patrons" so they started expressing their own emotions in their music and they stopped trying so hard.
   c. They started expressing their own emotions. In their music they stopped trying so hard. They stopped trying to please their "patrons."
   d. They started expressing their own emotions in their music, and they stopped trying so hard to please their "patrons."

7. What is the **best** change, if any, to make in the sentence in lines 24–25 (*Romantic composers . . . wealthy patrons.*)?

   a. Change *audienses* to **audiences**.
   b. Change *for* to **four**.
   c. Insert a comma after **composers**.
   d. Make no change.

8. Which of the following would be the **best** way to rewrite the sentence in lines 29–30 (*The music . . . twentieth century.*) to make it more specific?

   a. Although the music changed dramatically, even more radical changes would come later in the twentieth century.
   b. The music sounded very different from before, but much more radical changes would come later in the twentieth century.
   c. The music became more radical, emotional, but much more radical changes would come later in the twentieth century.
   d. The music had some similarities and differences, but much more radical changes would come later in the twentieth century.

9. What is the **best** change, if any, to make in the sentence in lines 7–8 (*People started . . . or society.*)?

   a. Change *individual* to **individuoal**.
   b. Change *to* to **too**.
   c. Change *then* to **than**.
   d. Make no change.

10. The sentence in lines 21–22 (*A patron . . . paying money.*) is poorly written. Which one of these is the **best** way to rewrite it?

    a. A patron was a very wealthy person who supported a musician he paid money.
    b. Who supported a musician paying money? A very wealthy person who was a patron.
    c. A patron was a very wealthy person supporting a musician who payed money.
    d. A patron was a very wealthy person who financially supported a musician.

I Deserve a Bigger Allowance

Kyle's seventh-grade class is learning how to write persuasively. Kyle's teacher asked him to think about something that he would like to have and then to write a letter to convince his parents that he deserves it. Kyle has written his rough draft, and now he needs your help editing and revising it.

Here is Kyle's rough draft. Read it and then answer questions 1–10.

1   Dear Mom and Dad,

2   I have been thinking a lot about finances lately, and I believe that I deserve a
3   bigger allowance. I know that you don't own the bank and that money doesn't grow
4   on trees, but I believe that I need more money. I will work to deserve the extra
5   money.

6   One reason that I need more money is that the cost of living has gone up. The
7   school cafeteria just raised its prices on the snacks I like to buy. The fines at the
8   library went up. Movies are more expensive. Even the swimming pool fee at the park
9   has gone up. I am in seventh grade now, so I am eating more than I used to. I'm also
10   doing more things. I like to practice at the batting cages play games at the arcade,
11   and go to the amusement park. I would like to have more of my own money to spend
12   on all these things.

13   Another reason that I need more money is that I would like to start really saving.
14   Its fun to spend money, but I would like to put more money into my savings account.
15   I know that you think saving money is important. If you gave me a bigger allowance,
16   I would have more money to put into savings.

17   It wouldn't be fair for me to ask you to give me extra cash every week without
18   giving you something in return. I plan to earn my bigger allowance by doing work
19   for you. You could give me work like mowing the lawn, cleaning the house,
20   babysitting, or doing odd jobs. After all, someday I'm going to have to know how to
21   do it all for myself. If you gave me more work to do. I would learn how to be more
22   responsible. You would have more free time, and I would have more money. Just
23   imagine it!

24   Please consider giving me a bigger allowance. I hope you agree that it would be
25   well worth the invessment.

26   Sincerely

27   Kyle

1. Which transition would **best** fit at the beginning of the sentence in lines 4–5 (*I will . . . extra money.*)?

    a. Therefore,
    b. For example,
    c. All kidding aside,
    d. Next,

2. What is the **best** change, if any, to make in the sentence in lines 10–11 (*I like . . . amusement park.*)?

    a. Change *amusement park* to **Amusement Park**.
    b. Delete the comma after **arcade**.
    c. Insert a comma after **cages**.
    d. Make no change.

3. What is the **best** change, if any, to make in the sentence in line 14 (*Its fun . . . savings account.*)?

    a. Delete the comma after **money**.
    b. Change *account* to **acount**.
    c. Change *Its* to **It's**.
    d. Make no change.

4. Where is there an incomplete sentence?

    a. in lines 24–25 (*I hope . . . the invessment.*)
    b. in line 6 (*One reason . . . gone up.*)
    c. in line 13 (*Another reason . . . really saving.*)
    d. in line 21 (*If you . . . to do.*)

5. What is the **best** change, if any, to make in the phrase in line 1 (*Dear . . . Dad,*)?

    a. Change the *comma* to a **period**.
    b. Change *Mom and Dad* to **mom and dad**.
    c. Change *Dear* to **Deer**.
    d. Make no change.

6. Which of the following would be the **best** way to change the phrase in line 26?

    a. Change *Sincerely* to **sincerely**.
    b. Change *Sincerely* to **Sinceerly**.
    c. Insert a comma after **Sincerely**.
    d. Make no change.

7. Which of the following is the **best** supporting detail to add after the sentence in lines 19–20 (*You could . . . odd jobs.*)?

    a. There are many things I could do.
    b. You could teach me how to cook, and I could make dinner sometimes.
    c. Working around the house wouldn't be so bad.
    d. The extra cash would be awfully nice to have.

8. What is the **best** way to rewrite the sentence in lines 8–9 (*Even the . . . gone up.*) to improve the paragraph?

    a. Even the swimming pool fee at the park isn't cheap.
    b. Even the swimming pool fee at the park has increased.
    c. The swimming pool fee at the park, even, has gotten more costly.
    d. It even costs more to go to the park swimming pool.

9. The sentence in lines 4–5 (*I will . . . extra money.*) is poorly written. Which one of these is the **best** way to rewrite it?

    a. I will earn the extra money I deserve.
    b. I deserve the extra money, and I will work.
    c. I will work, I will get extra money.
    d. I am willing to work to earn the extra money.

10. What is the **best** change, if any, to make in the sentence in line 24–25 (*I hope . . . the invessment.*)?

    a. Change *well* to **good**.
    b. Change *hope* to **hoped**.
    c. Change *invessment* to **investment**.
    d. Make no change.

LYME DISEASE

Alicia is in the seventh grade. Her teacher asked each student to choose one disease that humans can get from insects or animals and to write a short report about it. Alicia chose to write about Lyme disease. She took notes, organized them, and wrote her rough draft. Now she needs your help editing and revising it.

Here is Alicia's rough draft. Read it and then answer questions 1–10.

1 If you live in the northeastern United States, you definitely have heard of Lyme
2 disease. Before 1977, nobody knew about Lyme disease. Then, a group of children in
3 the town of Lyme Connecticut, started developing painful arthritis. When scientists
4 investigated, they found that all the children had been infected with a bacterium,
5 *Borrelia burgdorferi*. They found that people were getting this bacterium by being
6 bitten by deer ticks.

7 The deer ticks that carry the infection are much smaller than ordinary ticks found
8 on some animals. They feed by inserting there mouths into the skin of their hosts
9 and slowly taking in the hosts' blood. A tick can feed on its host for several days. The
10 longer it keeps feeding, the more likely it is to transmit Lyme disease.

11 The symptoms of Lyme disease include a round, red rash at the site of the bite,
12 headaches, fever, and pain in the joints and muscles. Sometimes people with Lyme
13 disease have a lot of itching. Some people develop heart problems or neurological
14 problems.

15 The people most at risk for getting Lyme disease are those living in the
16 northeastern states. However, there have been some cases in the mid-atlantic states
17 and parts of California, too. People who spend a lot of time outdoors are at higher
18 risk than those who don't. People who go in the woods a lot are especially at risk.

19 What if you love hiking and camping! It's not always possible to avoid places
20 where there are deer ticks. There are things you can do to keep from getting Lyme
21 disease. You can wear long-sleeved shirts and tuck your pants into you're socks. You
22 can wear light-colored clothes so that you can see ticks that jump on you. If you have
23 exposed skin, you can apply insect repellent that contains DEET. You can apply
24 permethrin to your clothes, too. Permethrin kills ticks on contact. Probably the most
25 important thing is to do a daily tick check. If you can find a tick that has been there
26 for just a day and remove it with tweezers. You probably will not get Lyme disease.

27 If you do get Lyme disease, you should get started on antibiotics immediately. If
28 you catch them early, Lyme disease can be cured.

1. What is the **best** change, if any, to make in the sentence in lines 16–17 (*However, there . . . California, too.*)?

   a. Change *have* to **has**.
   b. Delete the comma after **However**.
   c. Change *mid-atlantic* to **mid-Atlantic**.
   d. Make no change.

2. Which of the following would be the **best** way to rewrite the sentence in lines 7–8 (*The deer . . . some animals.*) to make it more specific?

   a. The deer ticks that carry the infection are much smaller than ordinary ticks found on farms.
   b. The deer ticks that carry the infection are much smaller than ordinary ticks found on dogs, cats, and cattle.
   c. The deer ticks that carry the infection are much smaller than ordinary ticks found on various animals around town.
   d. The deer ticks that carry the infection are much smaller than ordinary ticks found in the summer.

3. What is the **best** change, if any, to make in the sentence in lines 27–28 (*If you . . . be cured.*)?

   a. Change *disease* to **Disease**.
   b. Change *them* to **it**.
   c. Change *cured* to **kured**.
   d. Make no change.

4. What is the **best** change, if any, to make in the sentence in lines 2–3 (*Then, a . . . painful arthritis.*)?

   a. Change *arthritis* to **Arthritis**.
   b. Change *Then* to **Than**.
   c. Insert a comma after **Lyme**.
   d. Make no change.

5. What is the **best** change, if any, to make in the sentence in line 21 (*You can . . . you're socks.*)?

   a. Change *you're* to **your**.
   b. Change *tuck* to **tucked**.
   c. Insert a comma after **long-sleeved**.
   d. Make no change.

6. What is the **best** way to combine the two sentences in lines 17–18 (*People who . . . who don't.*)?

   a. People who spend a lot of time outdoors are at higher risk, but so are people who go in the woods.
   b. People who go in the woods and spend time outdoors are especially at risk.
   c. By going in the woods and spending time outdoors, the risks are especially high, but especially if you spend a lot of time in the woods.
   d. People who spend a lot of time outdoors, especially in or near the woods, are at higher risk than those who don't.

7. What is the **best** change, if any, to make in the sentence in lines 8–9 (*They feed . . . hosts' blood.*)?

   a. Change *hosts'* to **host's**.
   b. Insert a comma after **slowly**.
   c. Change *there* to **their**.
   d. Make no change.

8. Where is there an incomplete sentence?

   a. in lines 25–26 (*If you . . . with tweezers.*)
   b. in line 9 (*A tick . . . several days.*)
   c. in line 2 (*Before 1977 . . . Lyme disease.*)
   d. in line 13–14 (*Some people . . . neurological problems.*)

9. What is the **best** change, if any, to make in the sentence in line 19 (*What if . . . and camping!*)?

   a. Insert a comma after **hiking**.
   b. Change *you* to **me**.
   c. Change the *exclamation point* to a **question mark**.
   d. Make no change.

10. The sentence in lines 12–13 (*Sometimes people . . . of itching.*) is poorly written. Which one of these is the **best** way to rewrite it?

    a. Sometimes, when there's itching, people have Lyme disease.
    b. Sometimes, people with Lyme disease experience considerable itching.
    c. Even if it's a lot of itching, Lyme disease comes with people.
    d. Sometimes, people with Lyme disease have a bunch of itching.

SOUTH KOREA

Jacob is in the seventh grade. His geography teacher asked each student to choose a country and to write a short report describing the land and the people there. Jacob chose to write about South Korea. He researched his subject, organized his notes, and wrote his rough draft. Now he needs your help editing and revising it.

Here is Jacob's rough draft. Read it and then answer questions 1–10.

1　　　The Republic of Korea is commonly known as South Korea. It is located in the
2　southern half of the Korean peninsula in East Asia. The Democratic Republic of
3　Korea which lies to the north, is known as North Korea. These two countries used to
4　be a single nation. Then, in 1948, the world's super powers divided the country into
5　a communist North and non-communist South. The capital of South Korea is Seoul,
6　and it is also the largest city in the country. In the year 2000, there were 10.4 million
7　people living in Seoul, which makes it the most populated city in the world (if you
8　don't count major metropolitan areas.)

9　　　The Korean peninsula is located between the Yellow Sea and the Sea of Japan.
10　The east china sea lies to the south. The southeastern landscape is very dramatic.
11　It has mountain ranges that have deep, narrow valleys between them. The
12　southwestern part of the country is mostly coastal plains, and this is where most of
13　the people live.

14　　　South Korea has a temperate climate, but sometimes it gets bitterly cold during
15　the winter. There is a short rainy season every summer.

16　　　The Korean population is one of the least diferce groups of people in the world.
17　Except for a small Chinese community, most people in Korea are of the same ethnic
18　group and speak the same language. Koreans have friendly relationships with the
19　United States and Canada. Many Koreans who leave their country choose to come to
20　North America.

21　　　The Korean language has a writing system that is unique. In 1446, King Sejong
22　the Great invented it and called it the "Hangul." In this system, words are spelled
23　exactly as they sound. While Japan ruled Korea, people were forbidden to write or
24　speak the Korean language. Still, the language survived. Today, English is taught
25　as a second language in most Korean schools. When Korean students get to high
26　school, they can study Chinese, Japanese, French, German or Spanish.

27　　　The two most popular religions in South Korea are Christianity and Buddhism.
28　Before 1970, Buddhism dominated, but Christianity has overtaken it in recent years.
29　About thirty-five percent of South Koreans say they follow no particular religion.

30　　　In the last few years, South Korea and North Korea had considering reunification.
31　I wonder what'll happen.

1. What is the **best** change, if any, to make in the sentence in line 16 (*The Korean . . . the world.*)?

    a. Change *world* to **World**.
    b. Change *diferce* to **diverse**.
    c. Insert a comma after **population**.
    d. Make no change.

2. What is the **best** change, if any, to make in the sentence in lines 25–26 (*When Korean . . . or Spanish.*)?

    a. Change *high school* to **High School**.
    b. Insert a comma after **German**.
    c. Change *get* to **goes**.
    d. Make no change.

3. Which transition would **best** fit at the beginning of the sentence in lines 19–20 (*Many Koreans . . . North America.*)?

    a. Nevertheless,
    b. However,
    c. Then,
    d. In fact,

4. What is the **best** way to rewrite the sentence in lines 11–13 (*The southwestern . . . people live.*) to improve the paragraph?

    a. The southwestern part of the country, where mostly coastal plains are, is where most people live.
    b. People mainly live in the southwestern part of the country, which is mostly coastal plains.
    c. Coastal plains and people live in the southwestern part of the country.
    d. The country contains both coastal plains and people mostly in its southwestern part.

5. The sentence in line 21 (*The Korean . . . is unique.*) is poorly written. Which one of these is the **best** way to rewrite it?

    a. The Korean language is a writing system, which is unique.
    b. The unique writing system of the Koreans can be found in their language.
    c. The Korean language has a unique writing system.
    d. A writing system from the Korean language is unique.

6. What is the **best** change, if any, to make in the sentence in lines 2–3 (*The Democratic . . . North Korea.*)?

    a. Change *Democratic Republic* to **democratic republic**.
    b. Change *lies* to **lays**.
    c. Insert a comma after **Korea**.
    d. Make no change.

7. What is the **best** change, if any, to make in the sentence in line 10 (*The east . . . the south.*)?

    a. Change *east china sea* to **East China sea**.
    b. Change *east china sea* to **East China Sea**.
    c. Change *east china sea lies to the south* to **East China Sea lies to the South**.
    d. Make no change.

8. Instead of the sentence in line 31 (*I wonder . . . happen.*), which one of these uses the **best** tone for this audience?

    a. It will be interesting to see if these two countries ever join together again.
    b. I seriously doubt that will happen, but we'll see.
    c. South Korea and North Korea getting along? C'mon!
    d. It sounds like they've got a lot of problems to resolve first, though.

9. What is the **best** change, if any, to make in the sentence in lines 6–8 [*In the . . . metropolitan areas.*)]?

    a. Change *it* to **them**.
    b. Change *areas.)* to **areas).**
    c. Change *there* to **their**.
    d. Make no change.

10. What is the **best** change, if any, to make in the sentence in line 30 (*In the . . . considering reunification.*)?

    a. Change *considering* to **conssidering**.
    b. Delete the comma after **years**.
    c. Change *had* to **have been**.
    d. Make no change.

THE NEW SGA PRESIDENT

Tamara's seventh-grade class is getting ready to vote to elect new officers for the Student Government Association. Her teacher asked each student to choose one candidate and to write a letter to convince the class to vote for him or her. Tamara has written a rough draft of her letter, and now she needs your help editing and revising it.

Here is Tamara's rough draft. Read it and then answer questions 1–10.

1   Dear Fellow Classmates,

2   It is that time of year again: class elections! Have you decided whom you're voting
3   for yet? If not, please consider voting for Stephanie Hernandez. There are many
4   reasons why Stephanie is my favorite candidate.

5   Stephanie is, above all, a leader. She is not a follower of the crowd. People
6   sometimes don't do the right thing, but Stephanie always tell them that to their faces.
7   Whenever there is a chance to take charge, you will find Stephanie in the center of
8   the action. She is the captain of the girl's basketball team. She also helps teach
9   young children at her church. She has long brown hair. She has school spirit, too.
10   She is the person who thought of the design for our school anniversary pin.

11   Stephanie genuinely cares about other people. People go to Stephanie with their
12   problems. They know she will listen and won't laugh at them. Her advice is usually
13   very good, too. Stephanie does not play favorites or treat other people unfairly. If
14   anyone needs a helping hand, she is always the first one ready to offer her help.
15   When a student is out sick, Stephanie collects all the work, than explains it to the
16   student when he or she comes back.

17   I think Stephanie has another important quality that leaders need, and that's
18   humility. If she scores the most points in a game, she doesn't boast about it to
19   everyone and say, "Look how great I am!" When she is defeated, she accepts it with
20   grace and dignity. If somebody else doesn't do good, she encourages the person.
21   "Don't worry, I'm sure you'll do better next time" she will say. It's no wonder
22   Stephanie has a lot of friends. She makes the people around her feel good.

23   When it is time to cast your vote for class president on Tuesday, I hope you will
24   remember the name, Stephanie Hernandez. When it comes to representing our class,
25   I know she will do the best possible job.

26   Sincerely

27   Tamara Leonardo

1. What is the **best** change, if any, to make in the sentence in lines 15–16 (*When a . . . comes back.*)?

   a. Change *comes* to **came**.
   b. Change *than* to **then**.
   c. Insert a comma after **student**.
   d. Make no change.

2. Which one of these sentences does **not** belong?

   a. the sentence in line 22 (*She makes . . . feel good.*)
   b. the sentence in lines 2–3 (*Have you . . . for yet?*)
   c. the sentence in lines 11–12 (*People go . . . their problems.*)
   d. the sentence in line 9 (*She has . . . brown hair.*)

3. What is the **best** change, if any, to make in the sentence in line 21 (*"Don't worry . . . will say.*)?

   a. Change *you'll* to **you've**.
   b. Insert a comma after **time**.
   c. Change *Don't* to **don't**.
   d. Make no change.

4. Which of the following is the **best** supporting to detail to add after the sentence in lines 2–3 (*Have you . . . for yet?*)?

   a. Deciding who to elect for class president this year is going to be tough.
   b. I've made all my decisions already.
   c. The most popular kids always win.
   d. Student Government will be holding meetings on every other Thursday.

5. What is the **best** change, if any, to make in the sentence in line 23–24 (*When it . . . Stephanie Hernandez.*)?

   a. Delete the comma after **name**.
   b. Change *your* to **you're**.
   c. Change the *period* to a **question mark**.
   d. Make no change.

6. Instead of the sentence in lines 5–6 (*People sometimes . . . their faces.*), which one of these uses the **best** tone for this audience?

    a. Stephanie tells them straight out what's wrong with what they are doing.
    b. Whenever people are doing something Stephanie doesn't think is right, she is not afraid to speak her mind about it.
    c. Stephanie tells it like it is, but she isn't afraid of people not doing the wrong thing.
    d. Stephanie is not afraid to tell you when you're doing something wrong, and she's been known to not do the right thing from time to time.

7. What is the **best** change, if any, to make in the closing in line 26 (*Sincerely*)?

    a. Change *Sincerely* to **Sinsereley**.
    b. Change *Sincerely* to **sincerely**.
    c. Insert a comma after **Sincerely**.
    d. Make no change.

8. What is the **best** way to combine the two sentences in lines 11–12 (*People go . . . at them.*)?

    a. Stephanie is often told people's problems and she listens and she doesn' t laugh.
    b. People tell Stephanie their problems knowing very well that she won't listen or laugh.
    c. People's problems are especially important to Stephanie to help her listen and laugh.
    d. People go to Stephanie with their problems because they know she will listen without laughing at them.

9. What is the **best** change, if any, to make in the sentence in line 20 (*If somebody . . . the person.*)?

    a. Insert a comma after **else**.
    b. Change *good* to **well**.
    c. Change *encourages* to **encourajes**.
    d. Make no change.

10. What is the **best** change, if any, to make in the sentence in line 8 (*She is . . . basketball team.*)?

    a. Change *captain* to **Captain**.
    b. Change *is* to **were**.
    c. Change *girl's* to **girls'**.
    d. Make no change.

Spay and Neuter—Please!

Simon has been asked by his seventh-grade teacher to write a convincing article in favor of spaying and neutering pets. This topic is something Simon feels strongly about, so he enthusiastically begins gathering information and visiting local shelters. He has taken extensive notes and written his rough draft. He needs your help editing it.

Here is Simon's rough draft. Read it and then answer questions 1–10.

1 Not enough people understand the cat and dog overpopulation crisis going on in
2 the United States today. The shelters in this country are overloaded with household
3 pets that people have given up or abandoned. Shelters do their best to support and
4 maintain successful facilities. The staff wants nothing more then to find good homes
5 for all the animals in their care. However, it would be a miracle if they could save
6 every animal that crosses their paths. One effective solution to this problem is
7 spaying and neutering pets.

8 People often treat their pets as material possessions instead of living things. Pet
9 owners' common excuses for not spaying or neutering their pets is that they have not
10 bothered to do it yet. What a shame! Domestic animals are given up to shelters for
11 too many reasons. Perhaps the owners were moving, a landlord would not allow pets,
12 or there were too many animals already in the household. Maybe the pet cost too
13 much to take care of, the owner was having personal problems, or he or she did not
14 have adequate facilities for the pet. Sometimes people say really dumb stuff like they
15 don't want to pay to board the animal while on vacation.

16 No matter what the excuse domestic animals are being "euthanized," or killed,
17 every day. At least 10 to 12 million animals are euthanized each year because there
18 aren't enough homes for them. As many as a million animals a month.
19 Unfortunately, shelters just cannot handle the influx of pets they receive.

20 The statistical data surrounding pet overpopulation in this country is shocking.
21 If an unaltered cat, for example, is living on the street, he will most likely reproduce
22 at will. In fact, two unaltered cats and all of their desendants can theoretically
23 number 450,000 cats total in just seven years. One unspayed female dog and her
24 offspring can produce 67,000 dogs in just six years.

25 Kittens and puppies are often taken to shelters because breeders were unable to
26 find homes for the littermates. Many animals are simply neglected or abandoned by
27 their owners or run away. Over half of the dogs and a little less than half of the cats
28 of the shelter population come to the facility unaltered. As many as 25% of shelter
29 animals are purebreds. The owners would have paid good money to get a purebred
30 animal. Why would they toss it away?

31 Perhaps more people would spay and neuter their animals if they knew the health
32 benefits to the pet. The simple truth is that pet owners should know the dreadful
33 consequences of the pet overpopulation problem. Not spaying or neutering animals

(continued on next page)

(continued from previous page)

> 34 is the main cause. Educate yourself and those around you about responsible pet
> 35 ownership and the importance of spaying and neutering. The information will save
> 36 lives!

1. What is the **best** change, if any, to make in the sentence in lines 22–23 (*In fact . . . seven years.*)?

   a. Change *their* to **they're**.
   b. Change *desendants* to **descendents**.
   c. Change *two* to **to**.
   d. Make no change.

2. The sentence in lines 26–27 (*Many animals . . . run away.*) is poorly written. Which one of these is the **best** way to rewrite it?

   a. Many animals are simply neglected, abandoned, run away from their owners.
   b. Many animals run away because they are simply abandoned by their owners.
   c. Many animals simply run away or are neglected or abandoned by their owners.
   d. Many animals abandon and neglect their owners because they ran away.

3. The topic sentence of the second paragraph is in the sentence in

   a. lines 11–12 (*Perhaps the . . . the household.*).
   b. lines 14–15 (*Sometimes people . . . on vacation.*).
   c. line 8 (*People often . . . living things.*).
   d. lines 10–11 (*Domestic animals . . . many reasons.*).

4. What is the **best** change, if any, to make in the sentence in lines 16–17 (*No matter . . . every day.*)?

   a. Insert a comma after **excuse**.
   b. Delete the comma after **killed**.
   c. Change *euthanized* to **Euthanized**.
   d. Make no change.

5. What is the **best** change, if any, to make in the sentence in lines 4–5 (*The staff . . . their care.*)?

    a. Change *their* to **they're**.
    b. Change *then* to **than**.
    c. Change *good* to **well**.
    d. Make no change.

6. Where is there an incomplete sentence?

    a. in line 30 (*Why would . . . it away?*)
    b. in lines 12–14 (*Maybe the . . . the pet.*)
    c. in lines 35–36 (*The information . . . save lives!*)
    d. in line 18 (*As many . . . a month.*)

7. Which transition would **best** fit at the beginning of the sentence in lines 28–29 (*As many . . . are purebreds.*)?

    a. Surprisingly,
    b. Fortunately,
    c. Nevertheless,
    d. For instance,

8. Instead of the sentence in lines 14–15 (*Sometimes people . . . on vacation.*), which one of these uses the **best** tone for this audience?

    a. It's incredible what some people come up with when they want to go on vacation, like saying they don't want to pay to board their animal.
    b. Sometimes, people will act like they don't even care when they're going on vacation and they'll tell you they don't want to pay to board their animal.
    c. Some people surrender their pets for more thoughtless reasons, such as not wanting to pay to board the animal while on vacation.
    d. Can you believe some of these excuses, like saying you don't want to pay to board you animal so you can enjoy a relaxing vacation!

9. Simon wants to add the following sentence to the last paragraph: *Dogs and cats have a greatly improved chance of living long, healthy, contented lives if they are spayed and neutered.* The sentence would **best** fit

    a. after the sentence in lines 35–36 (*The information . . . save lives!*)
    b. after the sentence in lines 34–35 (*Educate yourself . . . and neutering.*)
    c. after the sentence in lines 32–33 (*The simple . . . overpopulation problem.*)
    d. after the sentence in lines 31–32 (*Perhaps more . . . the pet.*)

10. What is the **best** change, if any, to make in the sentence in lines 25–26 (*Kittens and . . . the littermates.*)?

    a. Change *to* to **too**.
    b. Change *were* to **are**.
    c. Insert a comma before **because**.
    d. Make no change.

John Calvin

Jackson's seventh-grade history teacher asked the class to draw a parallel between something they are interested in and their studies of the sixteenth century. Jackson makes a discovery, does some research, makes an outline for his report, and writes his rough draft. He needs your help editing and revising it.

Here is Jackson's rough draft. Read it and then answer questions 1–10.

1 *Calvin and Hobbes* is one of the best known comic strips of the last twenty-five
2 years. Written and illustrated by Bill Watterson from 1985 to 1995, it was carried
3 in over two thousand four hundred newspapers. But did you know that Calvin, the
4 six-year-old boy in the strip, is named after sixteenth-century theologian John
5 Calvin?

6 John Calvin was born on July 10, 1509, in Noyon France. He was raised in a strict
7 Roman Catholic family. In fact, John's fathers' work in the local cathedral led him to
8 want John to be a priest.

9 Calvin traveled to Paris to study at the College de Marche when he was fourteen
10 years old. He studied just seven subjects: rhetoric (public speaking), geometry,
11 arithmetic, astronomy, music, logic, and grammar. While living in Paris, he changed
12 his name to Ioannis Calvinus, the latin form of John Calvin. (In French, his name is
13 Jean Calvin.)

14 By 1832, Calvin had published his first book, a commentary on *De Clementia* by
15 Roman philosopher Seneca. He had also made friends with some reformist
16 individuals, who, at the time, who were seeking change. Soon thereafter, he fled
17 Paris because of ties with those same reformers, who were becoming known for
18 lecturing and writing against the Roman Catholic Church.

19 For three years following his departure from Paris, Calvin lived in various places
20 under various names. He studied and preached. He began work on the first edition
21 of the *Institutes of the Christian Religion*. That book made him famous. With this
22 book, he permanently seperated himself from the Roman Catholic Church. Calvin's
23 writings would spread the ideas of "Calvinism" throughout Europe, and even across
24 the Atlantic to the New World. Soon, countries around the world would be learning
25 and adopting Calvinist principles.

26 Calvin was passing through Geneva when he was met by William Farel, a local
27 reformer. Farel invited Calvin to stay in Geneva and, sources say, threatened him
28 with God's anger if he did not. However, many people disagreed with Calvin's
29 theological viewpoints and the changes he and Farel had set out to make. In 1538,
30 both Calvin and his partner were asked to leave.

31 After moving to Strasbourg, Calvin was surprised when the Council of Geneva, in
32 1541, requested that he return to Geneva. He did, eventually, return and began work

(continued on next page)

(continued from previous page)

> 33 as a lecturer, preacher, and writer of commentaries, treatises, and further editions of
> 34 the *Institutes of the Christian Religion*. He founded a school for training children and
> 35 a hospital for the needy.
> 36   Calvin was not well liked by some and he was sometimes threatened or abused.
> 38 Later in life, Calvin suffered migraines, lung hemorrhages, gout, and kidney stones.
> 39 He sometimes had to be carried to the pulpit. When his friends worried him about
> 40 the amount of work he insisted on doing, Calvin responded, "What! Would you have
> 41 the Lord find me idle when He comes"?
> 42   John Calvin died on May 27, 1564. At his own request he was buried in a simple,
> 43 unmarked grave somewhere in Geneva.

1. What is the **best** change, if any, to make in the sentence in lines 11–12 (*While living . . . John Calvin.*)?

   a. Delete the comma after **Calvinus**.
   b. Change *latin* to **Latin**.
   c. Change *changed* to **changed**.
   d. Make no change.

2. What is the **best** way to combine the three sentences in lines 20–21 (*He studied . . . him famous.*)?

   a. He began work on the first edition of the *Institutes of the Christian Religion* that made him famous while he was studying and preaching.
   b. He studied and preached, he finished writing the *Institutes of the Christian Religion* that made him famous.
   c. The *Institutes of the Christian Religion* would make him famous, but he studied and preached, too.
   d. He studied, preached, and began work on the first edition of the *Institutes of the Christian Religion*, the book that made him famous.

3. What is the **best** change, if any, to make in the sentence in lines 39–41 (*When his . . . He comes"?*)?

   a. Change *What* to **what**.
   b. Change *comes"?* to **comes?"**.
   c. Change *insisted* to **insissted**.
   d. Make no change.

4. What is the **best** change, if any, to make in the sentence in line 6 (*John Calvin . . . Noyon France.*)?

   a. Insert a comma after **Noyon**.
   b. Delete the comma after **10**.
   c. Change *France* to **france**.
   d. Make no change.

5. The sentence in lines 15–16 (*He had . . . seeking change.*) is poorly written. Which one of these is the **best** way to rewrite it?

   a. He have made also some friends who were reformists and individuals that had changed.
   b. He and his friends were seeking change in a reformist way at the time.
   c. He had also made friends with some reformist individuals who sought change.
   d. He had also made friends with some individuals who were seeking change, called "reformists."

6. What is the **best** change, if any, to make in the sentence in lines 7–8 (*In fact . . . a priest.*)?

   a. Change *cathedral* to **Cathedral**.
   b. Change *want* to **wants**.
   c. Change *fathers'* to **father's**.
   d. Make no change.

7. What is the **best** change, if any, to make in the sentence in lines 3–5 (*But did . . . John Calvin?*)?

   a. Remove the comma after **strip**.
   b. Change *did* to **does**.
   c. Change *theologian* to **theologians**.
   d. Make no change.

8. What is the **best** change, if any, to make in the sentence in lines 42–43 (*At his . . . in Geneva.*)?

   a. Change *was* to **were**.
   b. Insert a comma after **request**.
   c. Change *a* to **an**.
   d. Make no change.

9. Which of the following is the **best** supporting detail to add after the sentence in lines 27–28 (*Farel invited . . . did not.*)?

    a. Calvin had not planned on staying, but felt that Farel's request was God's intervention.
    b. Calvin's father had told him later on in life to give up theology and turn to the study of law.
    c. Growing up in the presence of the local bishop and his family exposed Calvin to both the aristocracy and culture.
    d. While in Strasbourg, Calvin was quite content working among French Huguenots.

10. What is the **best** change, if any, to make in the sentence in lines 21–22 (*With this . . . Catholic Church.*)?

    a. Change *Roman* to **roman**.
    b. Insert a comma after **himself**.
    c. Change *seperated* to **separated**.
    d. Make no change.

SHOULD WE SEND PEOPLE TO MARS?

Juan's seventh-grade science class is learning about space travel. His social studies teacher asked each student to form an opinion about whether or not the United States should try to send people to Mars, and then to write a letter to the president to convince him to either accept or reject the idea.

Here is Juan's rough draft. Read it and then answer questions 1–10.

1   Dear Mr. President,

2   Space travel has always fascinated we Americans. When Neil Armstrong of the
3   *apollo 11* mission became the first person to step out of his ship and walk on the
4   moon, he called it a "giant leap" for all humankind. Now it seems like everyone is
5   talking about putting people on Mars. Some people even think that there will
6   someday be a colony on Mars. Others believe that it is not wise to spend so much
7   money on a Mars mission when there are so many problems in the world. I think
8   that a Mars mission is well worth the time and money.

9   A mission to put people on Mars would be good for the world. If we finally did get
10 to the, "red planet," we would learn things that we would never learn if we tried to
11 study the planet from a distance. No one knows the incredible things that might be
12 discovered by astronaut scientists if they could finally dig samples with their own
13 hands. Maybe they would find fossils and other evidence of life among the dust and
14 rocks. Who knows? There could be valyable things on Mars that we humans could
15 use for energy or medicine. If we learned how to live on Mars, it could become a place
16 where humans could go to live if anything ever happened to our own planet.

17   If you think a mission to Mars would be impossible think again. Our astronauts
18 could launch their spaceship from the International Space Station. Then, they would
19 land on a satellite orbiting Mars. From there, they would land on a station that
20 would be waiting for them on the surface of the planet. Other spaceships would have
21 been already delivered packages of food and water. The astronauts could dig wells
22 for more water beneath the surface of Mars, and they could use solar panels for
23 electricity. Plants for food could grow inside the station greenhouse.

24   It is true that sending people to Mars would cost a lot of money. It is true that
25 there are lots of things we have to deal with in the world. However, these problems
26 are very complex, and money is not always the best answer. You're wrong if you don't
27 think we should learn everything we can about Mars. Someday, our lives just may
28 depend on it.

29   Sincerely,

30   Juan Martinez

1. What is the **best** change, if any, to make in the sentence in lines 20–21 (*Other spaceships . . . and water.*)?

   a. Insert a comma after **food**.
   b. Change *packages* to **package**.
   c. Change *would have been* to **would have**.
   d. Make no change.

2. What is the **best** change, if any, to make in the sentence in lines 2–4 (*When Neil . . . all humankind.*)?

   a. Change *apollo* to **Apollo**.
   b. Insert a comma after **ship**.
   c. Insert a comma after **mission**.
   d. Make no change.

3. What is the **best** way to rewrite the sentence in lines 19–20 (*From there . . . the planet.*) to improve the paragraph?

   a. They would land on a station that would be waiting, but from there they would go to the surface of the planet.
   b. They would land on the surface of the planet on a station that had been waiting for them.
   c. From there, they would get to the surface of the planet and they would find a station waiting there.
   d. From there, they would travel to a station waiting for them on the planet's surface.

4. What would be the **best** way to rewrite the sentence in lines 24–25 (*It is . . . the world.*) to make it more specific?

   a. It is true that there are problems in the world.
   b. It is true that there are tons of things to worry about in the world.
   c. It is true that there is war, hunger, and disease in the world.
   d. It is true that there are things that should trouble us in the world.

5. What is the **best** change, if any, to make in the sentence in lines 14–15 (*There could . . . or medicine.*)?

   a. Change *us* to **we**.
   b. Change *There* to **Their**.
   c. Change *valyable* to **valuable**.
   d. Make no change.

6. Instead of the sentence in lines 26–27 (*You're wrong . . . about Mars.*), which one of these uses the **best** tone for this audience?

   a. Just because you're the president of the United States doesn't mean you get to make decisions about Mars.
   b. I think it would be tragic to pass up the opportunity to learn everything we can about Mars.
   c. We should study Mars and we might learn us something.
   d. Learning about Mars would be a good idea, not because we want to but because we should protect ourselves against alien invasion.

7. What is the **best** change, if any, to make in the sentence in line 1 (*Space travel . . . we Americans.*)?

   a. Change *we* to **us**.
   b. Change *fascinated* to **fassinated**.
   c. Change *has* to **have**.
   d. Make no change.

8. What is the **best** change, if any, to make in the sentence in lines 9–11 (*If we . . . a distance.*)?

   a. Change *learn things* to **learned things**.
   b. Delete the comma after **the**.
   c. Insert a comma after **tried**.
   d. Make no change.

9. What is the **best** change, if any, to make in the sentence in line 17 (*If you . . . think again.*)?

   a. Change *would be* to **would have been**.
   b. Change *to* to **too**.
   c. Insert a comma after **impossible**.
   d. Make no change.

10. The sentence in lines 11–13 (*No one . . . own hands.*) is poorly written. Which one of these is the **best** way to rewrite it?

    a. By digging samples with their own hands, astronaut scientists might be discovered.
    b. Astronaut scientists might make discoveries with their own hands, but no one knows how incredible.
    c. Making discoveries, digging samples, and not knowing are all the incredible things that might happen if astronaut scientists use their own hands.
    d. If astronaut scientists could finally dig samples with their own hands, incredible things might be discovered.

A Hollow Earth

Trent's seventh-grade earth science class is studying scientific theories. His teacher asks each student to write a report on a topic that particularly interests him or her. Trent chooses the "hollow Earth" theory. He visits his school library and writes his first draft. He needs your help editing it.

Here is Trent's rough draft. Read it and then answer questions 1–10.

1 British astronomer Edmund Halley is usually mentioned in connection with the
2 comet that was named after he, Halley's Comet. Halley had some interesting
3 theories as well. Studying variations in the Earth's magnetic field led him to believe
4 that there were several magnetic fields. He thought that within the hollow Earth
5 were four spheres. One within the other and each with its own magnetic field.
6 Halley also believed that living creatures were inside this hollow globe. He thought
7 that the *aurora borealis*, or northern lights was created by the escape of a glowing
8 atmosphere through a thin crust at the North and South Poles. He proposed these
9 idea in 1692.

10 American John Symmes also supported this idea. He was a former army officer
11 and businessman. He believed that the Earth was hollow. He also believed that
12 there were four- to six-thousand-mile-wide entrances inside at the North and South
13 Poles. He raised money to make a expedition to the North Pole to explore the inner
14 Earth, but he was unsuccessful. After Symmes's death, a newspaper editor named
15 Jeremiah Reynolds helped to influence the U.S. government's decision to make such
16 an expedition to Antarctica in 1838. (This expeditions' findings did not support the
17 hollow Earth theory, but did lead explorers to conclude that Antarctica was the
18 world's seventh continent.)

19 Cyrus Read Teed first introduced the idea of human beings living within the hollow
20 Earth. He proposed that at the center of the hollow sphere was the sun, which was
21 half-dark and half-light. As the sun turned, it gave the appearance of sunrise and
22 sunset. The atmosphere in the center of the sphere was dense. Teed eventually
23 changing his name to "Koresh" and founded what was essentially a cult. He called
24 himself the messiah of a new religion, but died in 1908 without proving any of his ideas.

25 Even as late as World War II, Adolph Hitler may have sent an expedition to the
26 Baltic Island of Rugen because of these ideas. Once there, a scientist was told to
27 point a telescopic camera into the sky to try to photograph the British fleet across the
28 Earth's hollow center. (He was apparently unsuccessful). *UFOs—Nazi Secret*
29 *Weapons?* was written by Ernst Zundel. He suggested that nazis came from the inner
30 Earth. Zundel reported that Hitler went in a submarine to the South Pole where he
31 established a base for "flying saucers" in the hole leading inside the Earth.

32 Over time, new findings have made the hollow Earth theory seem silly. U.S. Navy
33 Admiral Richard Byrd flew across the North Pole in 1926. He didn't see any holes.
34 Then, he flew across the South Pole in 1929. He didn't see any holes then either. In
35 addition, astronauts' photographs show no openings at either spot.

1. Trent wants to add the following sentence to the last paragraph: *Therefore, people on one side of the world could not see those on the other side.* The sentence would **best** fit

   a. after the sentence in lines 14–16 (*After Symmes's . . . in 1838.*)
   b. after the sentence in lines 2–3 (*Halley had . . . as well.*)
   c. after the sentence in line 29 (*He suggested . . . inner Earth.*)
   d. after the sentence in line 22 (*The atmosphere . . . was dense.*)

2. What is the **best** change, if any, to make in the sentence in line 29 (*He suggested . . . inner Earth.*)?

   a. Change *inner* to **Inner**.
   b. Insert a comma after **from**.
   c. Change *nazis* to **Nazis**.
   d. Make no change.

3. What is the **best** change, if any, to make in the sentence in lines 8–9 (*He proposed . . . in 1692*)?

   a. Change *idea* to **ideas**.
   b. Change *proposed* to **propossed**.
   c. Change *He* to **Him**.
   d. Make no change.

4. What is the **best** change, if any, to make in the sentence in line 28 [(*He was . . . unsuccessful*).]?

   a. Change *apparently* to **aparently**.
   b. Change *unsuccessful).* to **unsuccessful.)**.
   c. Change *was* to **were**.
   d. Make no change.

5. What is the **best** change, if any, to make in the sentence in lines 6–8 (*He thought . . . South Poles.*)?

   a. Change *Poles* to **poles**.
   b. Insert a comma after **lights**.
   c. Insert a comma after **crust**.
   d. Make no change.

6. Where is there an incomplete sentence?

    a. in line 33 (*He didn't . . . any holes.*)
    b. in lines 22–23 (*Teed eventually . . . a cult.*)
    c. in lines 11–13 (*He also . . . South Poles.*)
    d. in line 5 (*One within . . . magnetic field.*)

7. What is the **best** change, if any, to make in the sentence in lines 16–18 [*(This expeditions' . . . seventh continent.)*]?

    a. Change *expeditions'* to **expedition's**.
    b. Change *to* to **too**.
    c. Change *world's* to **World's**.
    d. Make no change.

8. Which of the following is the **best** way to combine the four sentences in lines 32–34 (*U.S. Navy . . . then either.*)?

    a. In 1926 and 1929, U.S. Navy Admiral Richard Byrd flew across the North Pole and didn't see any holes.
    b. In 1929, U.S. Navy Admiral Richard Byrd flew across the South Pole, but in 1926, he flew across the North Pole and didn't see any holes.
    c. U.S. Navy Admiral Richard Byrd flew across the North Pole in 1926 and the South Pole in 1929 without seeing any holes leading inside the Earth.
    d. U.S. Navy Admiral Richard Byrd flew across both the North and South Poles in 1929 and 1926, and he didn't see any holes the first time and he didn't see any holes the second time either.

9. What is the **best** change, if any, to make in the sentences in line 13–14 (*He raised . . . was unsuccessful.*)?

    a. Change *was* to **is**.
    b. Change *a* to **an**.
    c. Change *explore* to **esplore**.
    d. Make no change.

10. What would be the **best** way to change the sentence in lines 1–2 (*British astronomer . . . Halley's Comet.*)?

    a. Change *Halley's* to **halley's**.
    b. Insert a comma after **connection**.
    c. Change *he* to **him**.
    d. Make no change.

THE NEW NEIGHBORS

Ellie's seventh-grade biology class has been studying zoology. Her teacher asks the class to write reports on animals or topics relating to animals. Ellie chooses her topic, researches it, compiles an outline, and writes her rough draft. She needs your help editing and revising it.

Here is Ellie's rough draft. Read it and then answer questions 1–10.

1 Imagine that your just sitting down to some eggs and bacon on a Sunday morning
2 when a coyote wanders past the kitchen window. This is becoming more common
3 every year as humans and animals are forced to share the same living space. In fact,
4 people are finding themselves living right alongside all kinds of wild animals.

5 This trend is no longer that unusual. Wildlife experts say that the human
6 population are expanding into areas where animals already live. Plus, by cleaning
7 up old parks and creating new ones, birds and animals are being drawn to areas
8 where people live. As human beings destroy wildlife's natural habitat, they will be
9 forced to share a living space. We all have to adapt somehow.

10 As it is, hundreds of thousands of whitetail deer currently live in suburban and
11 urban areas. The suburban coyote population is on the rise as well. Coyotes have
12 even learned to live in New York City's Central Park. They survive on garbage,
13 grubs, rodents, and pets. A family in Greenwich Connecticut, was surprised to find
14 that a family of foxes had built a den under their shed in the backyard. The mother
15 expected the foxes to be a nuesance and her first impulse was to drive them out.
16 However, after being advised to be tolerant, she learned that the red fox and her
17 "kits," or babies, were also a source of education for her family. She and her children
18 loved to watch the kits play. Once the babies had grown, the fox family abandoned
19 their den.

20 Often, a persons' fear will cause more trouble than it has to. For example, if a
21 bear or fox wanders onto someone's property the person may report to the authorities
22 that the animal has come to attack. In fact, the animal is probably just passing
23 through. If people protect themselves and their belongings—covering trash cans and
24 supervising household pets, for instance.

25 Not every human-animal interaction is necessarily good, however. Recently, a
26 mountain lion attacked a man and woman in a wilderness park outside of Los
27 Angeles. The man was killed and the woman was critically hurt. Nevertheless,
28 animal experts believe that such attacks are rare. People must be careful, but
29 wildlife will keep to themselves for the most part.

30 One thing we know for sure is that animals have learned to adapt to new
31 environments. Therefore, when wildlife arrives in a suburban or urban setting, they
32 will take advantage of sources of food and habitat. By taking the proper precautions
33 and using good judgment, while respecting the rights of wildlife, people can help
34 facilitate a harmonious living arrangement.

1. What is the **best** change, if any, to make in the sentence in line 20 (*Often, a . . . has to.*)?

    a. Change *to* to **too**.
    b. Change *persons'* to **person's**.
    c. Change *than* to **then**.
    d. Make no change.

2. What would be the **best** way to rewrite the sentence in lines 3–4 (*In fact . . . wild animals.*) to make it more specific?

    a. In fact, people are finding themselves living right alongside different animals.
    b. In fact, people are finding themselves living right alongside a variety of birds and animals.
    c. In fact, people are finding themselves living right alongside animals that come from many different places.
    d. In fact, people are finding themselves living right alongside deer, Canada geese, coyotes, foxes, bear, and moose.

3. What is the **best** change, if any, to make in the sentence in lines 32–34 (*By taking . . . living arrangement.*)?

    a. Delete the comma after **wildlife**.
    b. Change *judgment* to **judjement**.
    c. Change *us* to **we**.
    d. Make no change.

4. What is the **best** change, if any, to make in the sentence in lines 13–14 (*A family . . . the backyard.*)?

    a. Insert a comma after **in**.
    b. Insert a comma after **Greenwich**.
    c. Insert a comma after **den**.
    d. Make no change.

5. The sentence in lines 28–29 (*People must . . . most part.*) is poorly written. Which one of these is the **best** way to rewrite it?

   a. Wildlife will usually keep to themselves, but people should always be careful.
   b. People must be careful of wildlife keeping to themselves.
   c. Wildlife, who are keeping to themselves, are looking out for people who are trying to be careful.
   d. People must be careful because wildlife will keep to themselves for the most part.

6. What is the **best** change, if any, to make in the sentence in line 5–6 (*Wildlife experts . . . already live.*)?

   a. Change *live* to **lives**.
   b. Insert a comma after **say**.
   c. Change *are* to **is**.
   d. Make no change.

7. Where is there an incomplete sentence?

   a. in lines 1–2 (*Imagine that . . . kitchen window.*)
   b. in lines 12–13 (*They survive . . . and pets.*)
   c. in lines 23–24 (*If people . . . for instance.*)
   d. in lines 30–31 (*One thing . . . new environments.*)

8. What is the **best** change, if any, to make in the sentence in lines 20–22 (*For example . . . to attack.*)?

   a. Change *someone's* to **someones'**.
   b. Insert a comma after **property**.
   c. Change *has* to **have**.
   d. Make no change.

9. What is the **best** change, if any, to make in the sentence in lines 1–2 (*Imagine that . . . kitchen window.*)?

   a. Change *wanders* to **wander**.
   b. Change *Sunday* to **sunday**.
   c. Change *your* to **you're**.
   d. Make no change.

10. What is the **best** change, if any, to make in the sentence in lines 14–15 (*The mother . . . them out.*)?

    a. Change *her* to **she**.
    b. Change *nuesance* to **nuisance**.
    c. Insert quotation marks after **impulse**.
    d. Make no change.

POETIC PEACE

Heather's seventh-grade English class is studying poetry. Her teacher asks her to write a report on an important poet and his or her message. Heather reads the newspaper, does some brainstorming, and writes her first draft. She needs your help editing and revising it.

Here is Heather's rough draft. Read it and then answer questions 1–10.

1 Poet Mattie Stepanek faced challenges and hardships throughout his life. He was
2 known as a "peacemaker and poet, and his poetry celebrates the power of peace in a
3 difficult world. Stepanek was born with a rare neuromuscular disorder, a form of
4 muscular dystrophy. His illness did not stop him from spreading his message of
5 peace.

6 Stepanek started writing poetry at the age of three. He wrote to help him work
7 through his feelings about his disease, which caused muscle weakness as well as
8 difficulties with heart rate and breathing. He survived with the help of a power
9 wheelchair, ventilator, and supplemental oxygen. Stepanek's mother Jeni developed
10 a milder version of the disease after giving birth to her four children and the family
11 lost two brothers and a sister to it.

12 Stepanek was inspired to write about the power of love and peace. When he
13 appeared on the Oprah Winfrey Show, he told the audience that he expressed his
14 thoughts and feelings through writing. The audience was mostly women. "You're
15 heartsong is your inner beauty," said Stepanek. "it's the song in your heart that
16 wants you to help make yourself a better person, and to help other people do the
17 same. Everybody has one." This loving message helped to turn his five published
18 poetry books into bestsellers. They include *Heartsongs*, *Hope Through Heartsongs*,
19 and *Celebrate Through Heartsongs*.

20 Stepanek had the honor of meeting and establishing a friendship with the former
21 president, Jimmy Carter, who is also an advocate for peace. Him and Carter may even
22 have been working on a book about peacemaking together. Before the war in Iraq,
23 Stepanek sent a poem to president George W. Bush, asking him to seek peace. "We
24 cannot get caught with a bad attitude or we are not choosing peace," it read in part.

25 Stepanek served as the National Goodwill Ambassador for the Muscular
26 Dystrophy Association. He also excelled in his educational pursuits and earned a
27 junior black belt in martial arts. He once said, "I want people to know my life
28 philosophy, to remember to play after every storm."

29 Mattie Stepanek died on June 22 2004, in Washington, D.C. Nonetheless,
30 muscular dystrophy could never silence his message of peace and love. It's too bad
31 he had to die because his message seemed like a good one. July 14, 2004, would have
32 been his fourteenth birthday.

1. The sentence in lines 9–11 (*Stepanek's mother . . . to it.*) is poorly written. Which one of these is the **best** way to rewrite it?

    a. Stepank's mother developed a milder version of the disease, after giving birth to her four children, Jeni, two brothers, and a sister.
    b. Stepaneks' mother Jeni, developed a milder version of the disease, after giving birth to her four childrren, and the family, lost two brothers, and a sister to it.
    c. Stepanek's mother, Jeni, developed a milder version of the disease after giving birth to her four children, and the family lost two brothers and a sister to it.
    d. Stepaneks' developed a milder version of the disease from his mother, Jeni, who then gave it to her two brothers and a sister.

2. What is the **best** change, if any, to make in the sentence in lines 15–17 (*"it's the . . . the same.*)?

    a. Change *it's* to **its**.
    b. Insert quotation marks after **same**.
    c. Change *it's* to **It's**.
    d. Make no change.

3. Which transition would **best** fit at the beginning of the sentence in lines 4–5 (*His illness . . . of peace.*)?

    a. For example,
    b. Nonetheless,
    c. Then,
    d. Sadly,

4. What is the **best** change, if any, to make in the sentence in lines 21–22 (*Him and . . . peacemaking together.*)?

    a. Change *Him* to **He**.
    b. Change *have* to **having**.
    c. Change the *period* to an **exclamation point**.
    d. Make no change.

5. What is the **best** change, if any, to make in the sentence in lines 22–23 (*Before the . . . seek peace.*)?

    a. Delete the comma after **Bush**.
    b. Change *war* to **War**.
    c. Change *president* to **President**.
    d. Make no change.

6. Which one of these sentences does **not** belong?

    a. the sentence in line 31–32 (*July 14 . . . fourteenth birthday.*)
    b. the sentence in lines 26–27 (*He also . . . martial arts.*)
    c. the sentence in line 1 (*Poet Mattie . . . his life.*)
    d. the sentence in line 14 (*The audience . . . mostly women.*)

7. What is the **best** change, if any, to make in the sentence in lines 1–3 (*He was . . . difficult world.*)?

    a. Insert quotation marks after **poet,**.
    b. Change *world* to **World**.
    c. Change *difficult* to **dificult**.
    d. Make no change.

8. Instead of the sentence in lines 30–31 (*It's too . . . good one.*), which one of these uses the **best** tone for this audience?

    a. He had a good message to spread, but unfortunately he died.
    b. Our country is lucky to have known—even for a short while—such a brave, honest, and gifted poet.
    c. He died without having spread his message very far, which is really too bad.
    d. It's awful that he had to die, since it seems like we could have used his message for a while longer.

9. What is the **best** change, if any, to make in the sentence in lines 14–15 (*"You're heartsong . . . said Stepanek.*)?

    a. Change *your* to **you're**.
    b. Change *You're* to **Your**.
    c. Delete the comma after **beauty**.
    d. Make no change.

10. What is the **best** change, if any, to make in the sentence in line 29 (*Mattie Stepanek . . . Washington, D.C.*)?

   a. Change *D.C.* to **d.c.**
   b. Delete the comma after **Washington**.
   c. Insert a comma after **22**.
   d. Make no change.

SOME HIDDEN JEWELS

Noah has been asked by his seventh-grade English teacher to write a persuasive report on a subject relating to summer vacations. Noah brainstorms some of his ideas and draws up an outline. He has written his rough draft, but needs your help editing and revising it.

Here is Noah's rough draft. Read it and then answer questions 1–10.

1 When you're out looking for summer fun this season, try something a little
2 different. The popular national parks like yosemite, old faithful, and grand canyon
3 aren't all there is to see. In fact, the National Park Service manages three hundred
4 and eighty-eight national parks, seashores, monuments, and historic sites. Get out
5 there and explore them?

6 Dinosaur National Monument in Colorado is wonderful. It includes a "Dinosaur
7 Quarry," where visitors can see fossils and bones, as well as caves with rock art. Not
8 interested in giant extinct lizards? You can also go whitewater rafting down the
9 Yampa and Green Rivers camping, hiking, or biking.

10 If you're looking for something along the coast, Biscayne National Park in Florida
11 is an 175,000-acre oasis. It features water and living coral reefs. In Georgia,
12 Cumberland Island National Seashore offers sparkling beaches and dunes, maritime
13 forests, salt marshes, and freshwater lakes. Hike along the public paths or visit the
14 former vacation homes of the famous Carnegie and Rockefeller families. Sleeping
15 Bear Dunes National Lakeshore in Michigan was a U.S. Coast Guard rescue station
16 during World War II. If you visit today, you can watch reenactments of rescue crews
17 saving shipwreck victims. That's not all.

18 State parks offer another option this summer. I live in the state of Nevada. The
19 "Grand Canyon of the East," for example, is Letchworth State Park in New York.
20 Here you can find the Genesee River flowing amid six-hundred-foot-high cliffs.
21 Wisconsin's Copper Falls State Park features ancient lava flows, deep gorges, and
22 spectacular waterfalls.

23 Not even rainy weather can stop you this year. Rainy-day activities are there for
24 entertainment. Get involved in audio-visual programs, archeological exhibits,
25 museums, guided and self-guided tours, and demonstrations. Another alternative is
26 to pack rainy-day gear, so you can experience the park in wet weather. (All kids like
27 playing in the mud.)

28 Why would you want to explore something new? These parks are perfect for
29 families with small children because there less crowded and less stressful for
30 parents. Plus, they're often more affordable in terms of camping fees and entrance
31 fees. You should know that some small parks do not have all the things large parks
32 do. Some of the smaller parks may not offer flushing toilets, cold running water, or
33 facilities for RVs. Call ahead to be sure.

(continued on next page)

(continued from previous page)

> 34 Families can find these little known parks by visiting the National Park Service
> 35 website (www.nps.gov). Make an effort this summer to find a new "favorite vacation
> 36 spot.

1. The sentence in lines 23–24 (*Rainy-day activities . . . for entertainment.*) is poorly written. Which one of these is the **best** way to rewrite it?

   a. Rainy-day activities are entertaining there.
   b. Entertaining activities, such as rainy-day activities, are there for your entertainment.
   c. There are rainy-day activities at many parks, which are entertaining.
   d. Plenty of parks have rainy-day activities planned to keep you and your family entertained.

2. What is the **best** change, if any, to make in the sentence in lines 4–5 (*Get out . . . explore them?*)?

   a. Change the *question mark* to an **exclamation point**.
   b. Change *there* to **their**.
   c. Change *Get* to **Got**.
   d. Make no change.

3. What is the **best** change, if any, to make in the sentence in lines 8–9 (*You can . . . or biking.*)?

   a. Change *Rivers* to **rivers**.
   b. Insert a comma after **Rivers**.
   c. Change *can* to **been**.
   d. Make no change.

4. Which one of these sentences does **not** belong?

   a. the sentence in line 18 (*I live . . . of Nevada.*)
   b. the sentence in line 23 (*Not even . . . this year.*)
   c. the sentence in lines 2–3 (*The popular . . . to see.*)
   d. the sentence in lines 30–31 (*Plus, they're . . . entrance fees.*)

5. What is the **best** change, if any, to make in the sentence in lines 10–11 (*If you're . . . 175,000-acre oasis.*)?

    a. Change *you're* to **your**.
    b. Change *an* to **a**.
    c. Insert a comma after **Florida**.
    d. Make no change.

6. Which of the following is the **best** supporting detail to add after the sentence in line 17 (*That's . . . all.*)?

    a. The U.S. Coast Guard is helpful across the nation.
    b. There's more than just reenactments at Sleeping Bear Dunes National Lakeshore.
    c. Visitors can also swim, snorkel, scuba dive, fish, hike, kayak, and camp.
    d. This park is in Michigan.

7. What is the **best** change, if any, to make in the sentence in lines 2–3 (*The popular . . . to see.*)?

    a. Change *yosemite, old faithful, and grand canyon* to **Yosemite, Old Faithful, and Grand Canyon**.
    b. Change *is* to **are**.
    c. Change *there* to **they're**.
    d. Make no change.

8. What is the **best** change, if any, to make in the sentence in lines 35–36 (*Make an . . . vacation spot.*)?

    a. Insert quotation marks after **spot.**
    b. Change *to* to **two**.
    c. Insert a comma after **new**.
    d. Make no change.

9. What is the **best** change, if any, to make in the sentence in lines 28–30 (*These parks . . . for parents.*)?

    a. Change *are* to **were**.
    b. Insert a comma after **children**.
    c. Change *there* to **they're**.
    d. Make no change.

10. Which of the following is the **best** way to combine the two sentences in lines 31–33 (*You should . . . for RVs.*)?

    a. All small parks are missing some of the things that large parks have, such as flushing toilets, cold running water, or facilities for RVs.
    b. Flushing toilets, cold running water, or facilities for RVs can be found in small parks, but only when there aren't any large parks nearby that have flushing toilets, cold running water, or facilities for RVs.
    c. Large parks do have flushing toilets, cold running water, or facilities for RVs, but small parks don't have those things.
    d. You should be aware, however, that some of the smaller parks may not offer flushing toilets, cold running water, or facilities for RVs.

FROM PARAGUAY

Florence's seventh-grade social studies class is studying Latin American countries. Her teacher has asked each student to pretend he or she is from one of those countries and to write an imaginative story describing the culture. Florence chooses Paraguay, develops an outline, and writes her rough draft. She needs your help editing and revising it.

Here is Florence's rough draft. Read it and then answer questions 1–10.

1   Similar to the United States, outside groups helped to expand Paraguayan
2   culture. Spanish, Italians, Germans, Russians, Jews, Poles, Ukrainians,
3   Mennonites, Australians, Japanese, and small native tribes all contributed. Over
4   time, the groups became part of the country as a whole. Today, Paraguay is a diverse
5   and multicultural nation. It is the only officially bilinngaul country in Latin
6   America. Besides Spanish, close to ninety percent of the population speaks Guarani.

7   Folklore makes up the spiritual portion of the Paraguayan culture. Paraguayan
8   folklore is a combination of Hispanic cultures and smaller native tribes. Music,
9   dance, dresses, and food traditions are all tied to the country's folklore. When
10 visiting Paraguay, one may see religious festivals, fairs, and charity bazaars, which
11 are all part of the people's folklore traditions.

12 Music is very essential to Paraguayan customs. The polka appeared around 1856.
13 It is very different from European polkas. The Paraguayan polka is a happy,
14 rhythmic sound adopted from Spanish music. Jose Asuncion Flores created *guarania*
15 in 1925. This musical form emphasizes melody which makes it more for listening
16 than for dancing.

17 Paraguay's artisans are involved in many different skills and trades. Weavers
18 produce some of the finest silk, called *ñanduti* (or spider web silk). *Ñanduti* came
19 from the Canary Islands in Spain. It is often crafted into floral designs. Other
20 artisans weave wool, make cotton bedspreads, and craft ponchos. Some work in
21 leather, silver, and gold. Many craftsmen make baskets. The most famous *santeros*
22 are craftsmen who make religious images and objects. They mostly carve wood into
23 masks, crafts, and musical instruments.

24 Paraguay's cuisine shows the countrys multicultural roots. Their food varies from
25 homemade country food, always served with *chipas* (wheat rolls prepared with
26 manioc and cheese). To river fish and meat. Paraguayan food is one of the country's
27 most popular attractions.

28 Paraguayan sports are an important aspect of the country's culture as well. They
29 enjoy basketball, soccer, and other group sports. Soccer is the most popular sport.
30 The Paraguayan Soccer League was formed in 1906. Paraguay qualified for the
31 World Cups in Sweden in 1958, Mexico in 1986 France in 1998, and Korea in 2001.

32 Paraguay's multicultural identity influences all aspects of its traditions and
33 customs. The Paraguay of today were an ever-evolving gathering of the many
34 cultures that have chosen to settle there.

1. What is the **best** change, if any, to make in the sentence in line 24 (*Paraguay's cuisine . . . multicultural roots.*)?

    a. Change *shows* to **show**.
    b. Change *countrys* to **country's**.
    c. Change *cuisine* to **quisine**.
    d. Make no change.

2. What is the **best** change, if any, to make in the sentence in lines 9–11 (*When visiting . . . folklore traditions.*)?

    a. Change *may* to **won't**.
    b. Delete the comma after **bazaars**.
    c. Change *visiting* to **visited**.
    d. Make no change.

3. Mark wants to add the following sentence to the first paragragh: *Each group started out in a colony or a small settlement where it maintained its own customs.* The sentence would **best** fit

    a. after the sentence in lines 5–6 (*It is . . . speaks Guarani.*)
    b. after the sentence in lines 4–5 (*Today, Paraguay . . . multicultural nation.*)
    c. after the sentence in lines 2–3 (*Spanish, Italians . . . all contributed.*)
    d. after the sentence in lines 1–2 (*Similar to . . . Paraguayan culture.*)

4. What is the **best** change, if any, to make in the sentence in lines 33–34 (*The Paraguay . . . settle there.*)?

    a. Change *there* to **their**.
    b. Change *were* to **is**.
    c. Insert a comma after **ever-evolving**.
    d. Make no change.

5. The topic sentence of the second paragraph is in the sentence in

    a. the lines 9–11 (*When visiting . . . folklore traditions.*)
    b. the lines 8–9 (*Music, dance . . . country's folklore.*)
    c. the lines 7–8 (*Paraguayan folklore . . . native tribes.*)
    d. the line 7 (*Folklore makes . . . Paraguayan culture.*)

6. What is the **best** change, if any, to make in the sentence in lines 30–31 (*Paraguay qualified . . . in 2001.*)?

   a. Insert a comma after **1986**.
   b. Change *qualified* to **cwalified**.
   c. Change *World Cups* to **world cups**.
   d. Make no change.

7. Where is there an incomplete sentence?

   a. in line 13 (*It is . . . European polkas.*)
   b. in line 19 (*It is . . . floral designs.*)
   c. in line 26 (*To river . . . and meat.*)
   d. in line 29 (*Soccer is . . . popular sport.*)

8. What is the **best** change, if any, to make in the sentence in lines 5–6 (*It is . . . Latin America.*)?

   a. Change *bilinngaul* to **bilingual**.
   b. Change *Latin America* to **latin america**.
   c. Insert a comma after **officially**.
   d. Make no change.

9. What is the **best** change, if any, to make in the sentence in line 15–16 (*This musical . . . for dancing.*)?

   a. Change *than* to **then**.
   b. Insert a comma after **melody**.
   c. Change *emphasizes* to **imphasizes**.
   d. Make no change.

10. What would be the **best** way to rewrite the sentence in line 12 (*Music is . . . Paraguayan customs.*) to make it more specific?

    a. Paraguayan customs need music.
    b. Paraguay's folk music is one of the most impressive aspects of its cultural identity.
    c. Paraguay and music are essential to Paraguayan culture.
    d. Music is an essential part of Paraguayan customs.

GREEK FEMALE SLAVES   21

In her studies of ancient Greece, Mary found an interesting sidebar about Greek female slaves in her history textbook. When her seventh-grade history teacher asked the class to write a report on a topic pertaining to ancient Greece, Mary eagerly began writing her rough draft. She needs your help editing and revising it.

Here is Mary's rough draft. Read it and then answer questions 1–10.

    While a lot of information exists about Greek men's political military and cultural achievements we know little of the role of women in ancient Greece. What we do know comes from plays, philosophical texts, vase paintings, and sculptures (all created by males). Even the upper-class women were treated, by today's standards, as little more than slaves. We can only imagine how life for actual slave women (*thmoïs*) must have been due to they're gender and social status.

    Athenian women were broken down into three classes. The most low class was the slave women. The second class was that of the Athenian citizen women, who were the wives of the men in Greek society. The third class was known as the "hetaerae." The hetaerae were given an education in reading, writing, and music. They were allowed into the Agora and other places that were off limits to citizen and slave women. (For the most part, however, sources show that the hetaerae were no better then ancient prostitutes.)

    Slavery was common in the ancient world. Only in the poorest households were wives expected to do all the chores. These women also had to work in the fields or in stalls in the marketplace alongside men. Female slaves were usually the result of the spoils of a foreign war. It is unknown how much they cost. A document from 415 B.C.E. shows that the price of female slaves ranged from 220 drachmas to 85 drachmas. They were given many domestic tasks, such as shopping, getting wood, cooking and serving food, cleaning caring for children, and weaving wool. In wealthier households, some female slaves also worked as housekeepers, cooks, and nurses.

    An owner's personality and the slave's status determined how the slave was treated in the household. A female slave was often sexually and physically abused. Since female slaves were not allowed to raise their own children, any children born from a relationship between a slave and her master were done away with. Slaves could not even marry, since marriage were seen as a special privilege of the Athens elite.

    Although not required of them, slave girls often developed personal relationships with their mistresses. Upper-class women were kept isolated in their homes. They often turned to their slave girls for companionship. Female slaves went with their mistresses on outings as well. Tombstones with scenes of familiarity between the woman and her slave further display this bond. Both upper-class and slave women most likely drew closer together because of their exclusion from Athenian society.

(continued on next page)

(continued from previous page)

> 35 All women were allowed to participate in religion. In fact, religion was the only
> 36 public event all women could take part in. Slave women were included in some
> 37 religious affairs and could be initiated to the Eleusinian Mysteries, which celebrated
> 38 the myth of persephone.
>
> 39 Slavery was an important part of ancient Greek life. While an unfortunate truth,
> 40 perhaps the bonds women were able to form across social-class lines helped to justify
> 41 the struggle.

1. What is the **best** change, if any, to make in the sentence in lines 36–38 (*Slave women . . . of persephone.*)?

   a. Insert a comma after **affairs**.
   b. Change *initiated* to **inishiated**.
   c. Change *persephone* to **Persephone**.
   d. Make no change.

2. The sentence in lines 1–2 (*While a . . . ancient Greece.*) is poorly written. Which of these is the **best** way to rewrite it?

   a. While a lot of information exists about Greek mens' political military and cultural achievements we know lesser of the role of the womens' in ancient Greece.
   b. Information about Greek men's political, military, and cultural achievements is plentiful, while we know a lot less information of the role of women in ancient Greece.
   c. While much information exists about Greek men's political, military, and cultural achievements, we know little of the role women played in ancient Greece.
   d. Women and men in ancient Greece were political, military, and cultural, but we have little information on the role of women in ancient Greece.

3. What is the **best** change, if any, to make in the sentence in line 26–28 (*Slaves could . . . Athens elite.*)?

   a. Change *were* to **was**.
   b. Change *marriage* to **marryage**.
   c. Delete the comma after **marry**.
   d. Make no change.

4. What is the **best** change, if any, to make in the sentence in lines 7–8 (*The most . . . slave women.*)?

   a. Change *women* to **woman**.
   b. Change *most low* to **lowest**.
   c. Change the *period* to an **exclamation point**.
   d. Make no change.

5. The sentence in lines 33–34 (*Both upper-class . . . Athenian society.*) is poorly written. Which of these is the **best** way to rewrite it?

   a. Upper-class and slave women were probably drawn closer together because they were both excluded from Athenian society.
   b. Upper-class and slave women, both excluded from Athenian society, were drawn closer together most likely because they were excluded.
   c. Athenian society excluded upper-class and slave women, but that meant they were drawn closer together to Athenian society.
   d. They were both excluded, upper-class and slaves, but they were closer together, too.

6. Which transition would **best** fit at the beginning of the sentence in lines 25–26 (*Since female . . . away with.*)?

   a. For example,
   b. Then,
   c. Fortunately,
   d. However,

7. What is the **best** change, if any, to make in the sentence in lines 12–13 [(*For the . . . ancient prostitutes.*)]?

   a. Delete the parenthesis after **prostitutes.**
   b. Change *then* to **than**.
   c. Delete the comma after **however**.
   d. Make no change.

8. What is the **best** way to rewrite the sentences in lines 35–36 (*All women . . . part in.*) to improve the paragraph?

   a. Women could take part and participate in religion, but it was the only public event they could take part in.
   b. Religion was a public event. It was the only public event women could participate in.
   c. Women were allowed to publicly participate in religion, and that was the only thing they could do publicly.
   d. Religion was the only public event in which all women were allowed to participate.

9. What is the **best** change, if any, to make in the sentence in lines 5–6 (*We can . . . social status.*)?

   a. Change *they're* to **their**.
   b. Change *status* to **statuses**.
   c. Insert a comma after **imagine**.
   d. Make no change.

10. What is the **best** change, if any, to make in the sentence in lines 19–20 (*They were . . . weaving wool.*)?

    a. Delete the comma after **shopping**.
    b. Insert a comma after **cooking**.
    c. Insert a comma after **cleaning**.
    d. Make no change.

Two Respectable Men 22

Polly's seventh-grade English class has been working on their creative writing skills. Their teacher told them each to write a story that included setting, plot, characters, and details. Polly made a web of ideas and wrote her rough draft. She needs your help editing and revising the beginning of it.

Here is Polly's rough draft. Read it and then answer questions 1–10.

1   I'd been living in this little town called Burgsberg. It wasn't too far from anything
2   you might need, but it wasn't two close to anything either. I was sitting on the front
3   porch, taking stock of my apple orchards and smiling on the livestock. I had been
4   expecting a visit from the two men I most respect on this earth, Joe Frank and Mr.
5   Eddie West.

6   Now Joe Frank didn't expect a "Mr." at the front of his name since he had divorced
7   the former Mrs. Joe Frank and liked to keep it that way. He enjoyed the bachelor's
8   life and so we didn't burden him with all the business of being called "Mr." He
9   worked down at the mine as a foreman. He could fool you into thinking that someone
10 had outlined all the veins with a black pen under his skin because his skin creases
11 were so thickened with soot and his skin was so rough. We all figured his divorce was
12 the result of Mrs. Joe Frank being tired of washing soot out of she white bed sheets,
13 but no one had the courage to ask Joe if that was the case.

14 Mr. Eddie West, on the other hand, knew his business of being both a married
15 man and a man about the town. He worked in loans and securities at the National
16 Bank of Burgsberg. He could hold his own like any respectable village man. He
17 didn't like to brag about the fact that he had once taken down two young men in the
18 next town over. The boys had had fancy ideas about stealing Eddie's car. Now one
19 boy wishes he could go back to walking without a limp. The other boy dreams about
20 the day when hair will grow back over the bald spot Eddie gave him. That Mr. Eddie
21 West always was a tough guy.

22 As I said, I had been expecting these respectable men for a little under a half hour.
23 It was getting on toward dinnertime and I could smell the pork chops frying on the
24 stovetop. A warm breeze was lying on the tall, untrimmed grasses alongside the
25 porch. Even they seemed to know that the day was done.

26 The sound of an engine grew steadily louder and Joe Frank's 1963 chevrolet
27 Belair made its way up the driveway. My wife, Kristine, was calling me from inside,
28 but I knew that what Eddie, Joe, and I had to talk about was far more important than
29 any supper plate. I rose from the porch steps and met Joe at his driver's side door.
30 "Hello, Joe, I said, shaking his hand. "Eddie, how've you been?"

31 "Oh, I'm just fine, Dom," Eddie replied, climbing out from the other side of the car.
32 "What's this I hear about a proposition? The last time you came up with one of your
33 brilliant ideas, we all ended up in jail and I nearly lost my job at the bank."

(continued on next page)

(continued from previous page)

> 34   "Yeah, Dom," Joe said. "What's it about this time."
>
> 35   "This is pure, inspired genius this time, gentlemen," I assured them proudly. "I
> 36   thought of something last night and I've been waiting all day to tell you about it."
>
> 37   I know for a fact that, for all that they are respectable, Joe and Eddie may be the
> 38   least patient men in Burgsberg or anywhere else. I looked from one sober face to the
> 39   other, biding my time while hoping to pique their interests.
>
> 40   "You make me wait any longer, Dom, and I'll get right back in that car there,"
> 41   Eddie said as he turned to face Joe. "And you'll drive me home, Joe. Dom's news
> 42   can't be worth the spit its settling on."
>
> 43   "All right," I hastily said, not wanting to lose their attention. "Gentlemen, I
> 44   beleive I have come up with a way to . . . ," I began, allowing myself just one more
> 45   tiny dramatic pause before I continued, "to travel through time."

1. What is the **best** change, if any, to make in the sentence in lines 41–42 (*Dom's news . . . settling on.*)?

   a. Insert quotation marks before **Dom's**.
   b. Change *its* to **it's**.
   c. Change *be* to **been**.
   d. Make no change.

2. Which of the following is the **best** way to combine the two sentences in lines 18–20 (*Now one . . . gave him.*)?

   a. Now one boy wishes he could go back to walking without a limp, while the other boy dreams of the day when hair will grow back over the bald spot Eddie gave him.
   b. Now one boy goes back to walking with a limp and the other boy dreams about the day when hair will grow back over the bald spot Eddie gave him.
   c. Now one boy and the other boy dream of walking without a limp and about the day when hair will grow back over the bald spot Eddie gave him.
   d. Now one boy walks with a limp and the other boy has a bald spot.

3. What is the **best** change, if any, to make in the sentence in lines 11–13 (*We all . . . the case.*)?

   a. Change *being* to **was**.
   b. Insert a comma after **Frank**.
   c. Change *she* to **her**.
   d. Make no change.

4. Polly wants to add the following sentence to the seventh or eighth paragraph: *All the same, I wanted to give my news the proper weight by not blurting it out right away.* The sentence would **best** fit

   a. after the sentence in line 35 (*"This is . . . them proudly.*).
   b. after the sentence in lines 35–36 (*"I thought . . . about it."*).
   c. after the sentence in lines 37–38 (*I know . . . anywhere else.*).
   d. after the sentence in lines 38–39 (*I looked . . . their interests.*).

5. What is the **best** change, if any, to make in the sentence in line 30 (*"Hello, Joe . . . his hand.*)?

   a. Change *his* to **him**.
   b. Insert quotation marks after **Joe,**.
   c. Change *I* to **i**.
   d. Make no change.

6. What is the **best** change, if any, to make in the sentence in lines 1–2 (*It wasn't . . . anything either.*)?

   a. Change *two* to **too**.
   b. Delete the comma after **need**.
   c. Change the *period* to a **question mark**.
   d. Make no change.

7. The sentence in lines 9–11 (*He could . . . so rough.*) is poorly written. Which of these is the **best** way to rewrite it?

   a. His skin was rough, thickened by soot, and outlined with black pen under his veins, which he could fool you into thinking.
   b. He could fool you into thinking his rough skin was thickened with soot when in actuality it was outlined with black pen.
   c. Black pen and soot thickened his rough skin, all in the creases, but he couldn't fool you.
   d. The creases of his rough skin were so thickened with soot that he could fool you into thinking that someone had outlined all the veins under his skin in black pen.

8. What is the **best** change, if any, to make in the sentence in line 43–45 ("*Gentlemen, I . . . through time.*")?

    a. Delete the quotation marks before **to**.
    b. Change *beleive* to **believe**.
    c. Change *have* to **had**.
    d. Make no change.

9. What is the **best** change, if any, to make in the sentence in line 34 ("*What's it . . . this time.*")?

    a. Change the *period* to a **question mark**.
    b. Insert a comma after **it**.
    c. Change *What's* to **What are**.
    d. Make no change.

10. What is the **best** change, if any, to make in the sentence in lines 26–27 (*The sound . . . the driveway.*)?

    a. Change *grew* to **growed**.
    b. Change *its* to **it's**.
    c. Change *chevrolet* to **Chevrolet**.
    d. Make no change.

Circadian Rhythm 23

Zeke's seventh-grade biology class has been studying physiological processes. His teacher asks each student to write a report on one of the body's processes. Zeke visits the school library and writes his rough draft. He needs your help editing and revising it.

Here is Zeke's rough draft. Read it and then answer questions 1–10.

1 It is interesting that as it grows darker in the evening, we generally seem to get
2 more tired. Perhaps you've noticed that you have more energy at a certain point in
3 the day. A process, called a "circadian rhythm," is going on within we. The term,
4 circadian, comes from two Latin words: *circa*, meaning "about," and *dies*, meaning
5 "day." You may have heard it referred to as a "body clock."

6 Within the hypothalamus in our brains is a trigger that tells us that it is time for
7 sleep. A gland called the pineal gland is regulated by light that comes in through our
8 eyes. When there is less light, a hormone called melatonin is produced. When it gets
9 darker outside, melatonin levels increase in our bodies. A signal is then sent to our
10 hypothalamus and we get sleepy. When there is more light coming in through our
11 eyes, melatonin production decreases. When our eyes receive light, as in the
12 morning, our body clock resets itself. This entire process is a circadian rhythm.

13 Other elements of our daily routines also act to reset our body clocks. Physical
14 activity temperature, and social routines often play a part. Light and darkness are
15 the only factors that seem to consistently affect the rhythm of our bodies. In
16 experiments, the circadian rhythms of animals kept in total darkness for extended
17 periods of time became highly irregular.

18 Many problems can arise if your body clock malfunctions. If you have ever
19 experienced "jet lag" you know how it feels when your sleep/awake cycle is
20 interrupted. Fatigue, disorientation, and insomnia are all associated with these
21 kinds of interruptions. A disorder called "advanced sleep phase syndrome" causes a
22 person to feel listless in the evening, while sleeping longer in the morning. Blind
23 people often suffer from "hypernychthemeral syndrome." They will stay up later and
24 later every night and wake up later every morning after staying up late every night.

25 The most common disorder is "delayed sleep phase syndrome," or DSPS. Some
26 people who have DSPS think that they are night owls because they notice that their
27 minds work best at a later time than most people's and most of them fall asleep later
28 than normal, sometimes not until early morning. Since they usually fall asleep at
29 the same time every night, people with DSPS are actually on a schedule. Problems
30 will arise when they have to woke up early in the morning. Until 1981, when DSPS
31 was classified as a sleeping disorder, sufferers were just thought to be lazy.

32 Keeping your circadian rhythm intact is essential to being healthy. Avoid the
33 short-term negative affects of disrupting your sleep schedule and you will enjoy a
34 better, restfuller lifestyle.

1. The topic sentence of the fourth paragraph is in
    a. line 18 (*Many problems . . . clock malfunctions.*).
    b. lines 20–21 (*Fatigue, disorientation . . . of interruptions.*).
    c. lines 21–22 (*A disorder . . . the morning.*).
    d. lines 23–24 (*They will . . . every night.*).

2. What is the **best** way to rewrite the sentence in lines 23–24 (*They will . . . every night.*) to improve the paragraph?
    a. They will wake up later every morning, stay up later and later every night.
    b. They will stay up later and later, wake up later and later, stay up later and later.
    c. They will stay up later and later every night and wake up later every morning.
    d. They will wake up later after having stayed up later and later and later.

3. What is the **best** change, if any, to make in the sentence in line 3 (*A process . . . within we.*)?
    a. Change *a* to **an**.
    b. Change *we* to **us**.
    c. Change *rhythm* to **rithem**.
    d. Make no change.

4. What is the **best** change, if any, to make in the sentence in lines 29–30 (*Problems will . . . the morning.*)?
    a. Change *will* to **would**.
    b. Change *woke* to **wake**.
    c. Change *to* to **two**.
    d. Make no change.

5. What is the **best** change, if any, to make in the sentence in lines 13–14 (*Physical activity . . . a part.*)?
    a. Insert a comma after **activity**.
    b. Insert a comma after **Physical**.
    c. Delete the comma after **temperature**.
    d. Make no change.

6. The sentence in lines 25–28 (*Some people . . . early morning.*) is poorly written. Which one of these is the **best** way to rewrite it?

   a. Some people who have DSPS may think they work best at a later time like night owls, but then they fall asleep later than normal, sometimes not until early morning.
   b. Some DSPS people are night owls who work best at a later time than most, but they also fall asleep in the early morning.
   c. Some people fall asleep in the early morning, while others fall asleep later than normal. They all have DSPS like most people.
   d. Some people who have DSPS may think that they are night owls. Their minds work best at a later time than most people's. Most sufferers fall asleep later than normal, sometimes not until early morning.

7. What is the **best** change, if any, to make in the sentence in lines 18–19 (*If you . . . is interrupted.*)?

   a. Change *feels* to **felt**.
   b. Insert a comma after **lag**.
   c. Change *your* to **you're**.
   d. Make no change.

8. What is the **best** change, if any, to make in the sentence in line 32 (*Keeping your . . . being healthy.*)?

   a. Change *your* to **you're**.
   b. Change *an* to **a**.
   c. Change *being* to **been**.
   d. Make no change.

9. What is the **best** change, if any, to make in the sentence in lines 32–34 (*Avoid the . . . resfuller lifestyle.*)?

   a. Change *restfuller* to **more restful**.
   b. Change *your* to **you're**.
   c. Delete the comma after **better**.
   d. Make no change.

10. Which transition would **best** fit at the beginning of the sentence in lines 8–9 (*When it . . . our bodies.*)?

    a. For example,
    b. Now,
    c. Therefore,
    d. First,

MEDGAR EVERS

Gerry's seventh-grade history class is studying civil rights. His teacher asks the class to write biographies on men and women involved in civil rights in the twentieth century. Gerry chooses Medgar Evers, does some research, and writes his rough draft. He needs your help editing and revising it.

Here is Gerry's rough draft. Read it and then answer questions 1–10.

1   Medgar Wiley Evers was born on July 2 1925, near Decatur, Mississippi. He was
2   drafted into the army during World War II. When he returned home, he found that
3   he still couldn't drink from the same water fountains, eat at the same lunch
4   counters, or ride the same trains as white people. Evers's battle for civil rights had
5   begun.

6   In 1946, at Decatur's courthouse, Evers was turned away from trying to register
7   to vote. From 1954 to 1963, he served as field secretary for Mississippi in the
8   NAACP. He traveled throughout his home state, encouraging African Americans to
9   register to vote. He also fought for integrated schools and organized boycotts against
10 white-owned firms that practiced racial discrimmanation.

11 Although he faced daily hardship, Evers couldn't imagine leaving the southern
12 states. In a magazine article written in 1954, Evers said of the South, "I don't choose
13 to live anywhere else. There's land here, where a man can raise cattle, and I'm going
14 to do it some day."

15 It didn't take long for Evers to become a target for racists. On June 12, 1963,
16 Evers was shot and killed outside his home in Jackson Mississippi. Ten days later,
17 police arrested white supremacist Byron De La Beckwith for the murder. Two all-
18 white juries could not reach a verdict on the case. In 1969, the charges against
19 Beckwith were dropped. Twenty years later, the case was reopened with new
20 charges. In 1994, a jury of eight African Americans and four whites convicted
21 Beckwith of Evers's murder.

22 Demonstrators in the black community marched after Evers's funeral procession,
23 shouting, "After Medgar, No More Fear! Local resident Walter Gardner said that
24 this event made him realize the importance of acting for what you believe in. Doing
25 "something to be a participant and not a bystander in our society."

26 In 1969, Evers's brother, Charles, became the first African-American mayor to be
27 elected in Mississippi. In an interview with national public radio, Charles said,
28 "Medgar and I said many years ago, if we ever end the violent racism in this state,
29 it'll be the greatest state in the world to live. And now, Medgar, I know your gone,
30 but I'm telling you, son, it's come to pass."

31 Evers did a lot of stuff for African Americans. His legacy lived on long after his
32 assassination. When Medgar Evers died in 1963, only 28,000 African Americans
33 were registered to vote. Nearly twenty years later, there were over 500,000.

1. What is the **best** change, if any, to make in the sentence in lines 11–12 (*Although he . . . southern states.*)?

   a. Change *southern* to **Southern**.
   b. Delete the comma after **hardship**.
   c. Change *faced* to **faces**.
   d. Make no change.

2. Which of the following is the **best** supporting detail to add after the sentence in lines 16–17 (*Ten days . . . the murder.*)?

   a. It is not clear where Beckwith was from.
   b. Beckwith, whose fingerprints were found on the murder weapon, was tried twice.
   c. Segregation was an ongoing problem in Mississippi.
   d. Evers's brother, Charles, succeeded him as NAACP field secretary.

3. What is the **best** change, if any, to make in the sentence in line 1 (*Medgar Wiley . . . Decatur, Mississippi.*)?

   a. Delete the comma after **Decatur**.
   b. Insert a comma after **2**.
   c. Change the *period* to a **question mark**.
   d. Make no change.

4. What is the **best** change, if any, to make in the sentence in lines 22–23 (*Demonstrators in . . . More Fear!*)?

   a. Insert quotation marks after **Fear!**
   b. Change the *exclamation point* to a **period**.
   c. Insert a comma after **community**.
   d. Make no change.

5. Where is there an incomplete sentence?

   a. in lines 4–5 (*Evers's battle . . . had begun.*)
   b. in lines 12–13 (*In a . . . anywhere else.*)
   c. in line 33 (*Nearly twenty . . . over 500,000.*)
   d. in lines 24–25 (*Doing "something . . . our society."*)

6. What is the **best** change, if any, to make in the sentence in lines 29–30 (*And now . . . to pass."*)?

   a. Change *your* to **you're**.
   b. Delete the quotation marks after **pass**.
   c. Change *it's* to **its**.
   d. Make no change.

7. What is the **best** change, if any, to make in the sentence in lines 15–16 (*On June . . . Jackson Mississippi.*)?

   a. Delete the comma after **12**.
   b. Change *his* to **him**.
   c. Insert a comma after **Jackson**.
   d. Make no change.

8. Instead of the sentence in line 31 (*Evers did . . . African Americans.*), which of these uses the **best** tone for this audience?

   a. Mostly, Evers worked hard for African Americans.
   b. Evers struggled throughout his life to protect African Americans from discrimination and cruelty.
   c. Civil rights was an important issue to African Americans, so Evers probably cared a lot about it since he was an African American.
   d. I guess he did stuff for African Americans.

9. What is the **best** change, if any, to make in the sentence in lines 27–29 (*In an . . . to live.*)?

   a. Delete the comma after **state**.
   b. Change *to* to **too**.
   c. Change *national public radio* to **National Public Radio**.
   d. Make no change.

10. What is the **best** change, if any, to make in the sentence in lines 9–10 (*He also . . . racial discrimmanation.*)?

    a. Change *fought* to **fight**.
    b. Change *discrimmanation* to **discrimination**.
    c. Change the period to an **exclamation point**.
    d. Make no change.

The Best Sports Team Ever

James is in the seventh grade. His teacher asked him to decide which sports team he thought was the best team ever and to write a short essay to explain why he thought the team was so great. James chose to write about the New York Yankees.

Here is James's rough draft. Read it and then answer questions 1–10.

1 When you hear the names, Babe Ruth, Lou Gehrig, Joe DiMaggio, Yogi Berra,
2 Mickey Mantle, and Reggie Jackson what immediately comes to mind? The New
3 York Yankees, of course! The New York Yankees are, in my opinion, the greatest
4 baseball team in history and the greatest sports team ever.

5 The New York Yankees started out as the "Highlanders" because their first
6 stadium in New York sat on top of the highest hill in the city. They were officially
7 named the "Yankees" in 1913. In 1920, they bought Babe Ruth's contract from the
8 Boston Red Sox and started building Yankee Stadium. I wish I had having been
9 there for the opening game at the stadium. The Yankees beat the Red Sox 4–1, and
10 Babe Ruth—"the Bambino"—hit his first home run in the stadium in front of 74,000
11 people.

12 The Yankees have had some truly outstanding players. For example, Lou Gehrig
13 was the only player in major league history to hit twenty-three" grand slam" home
14 runs during his career. He averaged an incredible 147 runs batted in per year and, in
15 1931, he batted in a record 184 runs. He made "Most Valuable Player" twice and won
16 one Triple Crown. He also contracted a disaease called "Amyotrophic Lateral
17 Sclerosis," or ALS, when he was thirty-five years old. This disease was later called
18 "Lou Gehrig's Disease." When Lou Gehrig got sick, the Yankees retired his number
19 and gave him a big retirement party. His number—four—was the first number ever
20 to be retired in baseball. Even though he had a fatal disease and his baseball career
21 was over. Lou Gehrig felt so grateful and proud to be one of the Yankees that he told
22 everyone, "today I consider myself the luckiest man on the face of the earth."

23 So far this season, the Yankees have only lost three of their last twenty-one
24 games. They have a five-and-a-half-game lead over their rival, the Boston red sox.
25 Players like Derek Jeter, Gary Sheffield, Hideki Matsui, Alex Rodriguez, Mike
26 Mussina, Bernie Williams, and Jose Contreras are leading their team to victory.
27 There are many great ball players in the Yankees right now. There are so many that
28 the next All-Star game may have as many as five Yankees players in it. That's a
29 game I don't want to miss?

30 Because of their great history and all the talented players who are on the team
31 today, I think the New York Yankees are the best sports team ever. If I were a
32 professional baseball player, I would definitely want to go to work for the New York
33 Yankees.

1. What is the **best** change, if any, to make in the sentence in line 5–6 (*The New . . . the city.*)?

    a. Delete the quotation marks before **Highlanders**.
    b. Change *their* to **they're**.
    c. Change *highest* to **most higher**.
    d. Make no change.

2. Where is there an incomplete sentence?

    a. in lines 23–24 (*So far . . . twenty-one games.*)
    b. in lines 9–11 (*The Yankees . . . 74,000 people.*)
    c. in lines 3–4 (*The New . . . team ever.*)
    d. in lines 20–21 (*Even though . . . was over.*)

3. Which of the following is the **best** way to combine the two sentences in lines 27–28 (*There are . . . in it.*)?

    a. There are so many great ball players in the Yankees right now that the next All-Star game may have as many as five Yankees players in it.
    b. Many of the great ball players in the Yankees right now will be in the All-Star game, including five players that are in it.
    c. Five Yankee players are in the All-Star game, and there may be as many great ball players in the Yankees right now.
    d. The All-Star game will definitely have five Yankee players in it, but that doesn't count all the really good players that are on the Yankees right now.

4. What is the **best** change, if any, to make in the sentence in lines 16–17 (*He also . . . years old.*)?

    a. Delete the comma after **Sclerosis**.
    b. Change *disaease* to **disease**.
    c. Insert quotation marks after **ALS,**.
    d. Make no change.

5. What is the **best** change, if any, to make in the sentence in lines 8–9 (*I wish . . . the stadium.*)?

   a. Change *there* to **their**.
   b. Change *had having* to **had**.
   c. Insert a comma after **game**.
   d. Make no change.

6. What is the **best** change, if any, to make in the sentence in lines 21–22 (*Lou Gehrig . . . the earth."*)?

   a. Change *"today* to **"Today**.
   b. Delete the comma after **everyone**.
   c. Change *he* to **him**.
   d. Make no change.

7. What is the **best** change, if any, to make in the sentence in line 24 (*They have . . . red sox.*)?

   a. Delete the comma after **rival**.
   b. Change *their* to **there**.
   c. Change *red sox* to **Red Sox**.
   d. Make no change.

8. Which transition would **best** fit at the beginning of the sentence in lines 16–17 (*He also . . . years old.*)?

   a. Luckily,
   b. For example,
   c. Unfortunately,
   d. However,

9. What is the **best** change, if any, to make in the sentence in lines 28–29 (*That's a . . . to miss?*)?

   a. Change *don't* to **doesn't**.
   b. Change the *question mark* to an **exclamation point**.
   c. Change *That's* to **That was**.
   d. Make no change.

10. What is the **best** change, if any, to make in the sentence in lines 1–2 (*When you . . . to mind?*)?

    a. Change the *question mark* to a **period**.
    b. Delete the comma after **DiMaggio**.
    c. Insert a comma after **Jackson**.
    d. Make no change.

ISOLATIONISM *vs.* IMPERIALISM

Jutlee is in the seventh grade. Her social studies teacher asked each student to write an essay defining, isolationism and imperialism, two forms of foreign policy, and then contrasting the two. Jutlee did her research, made her outline, and wrote her rough draft. Now she needs your help editing and revising it.

Here is Jutlee's rough draft. Read it and then answer questions 1–10.

1 Imagine that you and your friend see two students having an argument on the
2 playground. You don't want to get involved because you think that the two students
3 should work it out by themselves. "Come on, let's walk away and mind our own
4 business," you tell your friend. We'll just make matters worse."

5 "No! We have to step in before somebody gets hurt. I know how to handle this,
6 and they need my advice" answers your friend. Did you know that you and your
7 friend are practicing "isolationism" and "imperialism"?

8 Isolationism is a policy that affects the way a country relates to other countries.
9 Isolationist countries don't believe in getting too involved with other countrie's
10 business or politics. They do not like to form alliances with other countries. They
11 try very hard to be self-sufficient, and they don't want other countries to depend upon
12 they. An isolationist country believes that if it just takes care of itself, they're will be
13 peace and prosperity. At the beginning of the twentieth century before World War I,
14 many people from the United States favored isolationism.

15 Imperialism is a policy that is the opposite of isolationism. Imperialist countries
16 get involved in the business and politics of other countries. They form economic
17 partnerships and they depend on the relationships they have with other countries.
18 If they don't like what a country's government is doing, they try to influence that
19 government. Several imperialist countries might work together for a common goal.
20 The United States and it's allies worked together to win World War II.

21 The United States practiced imperialism during the Vietnam War. President
22 Eisenhower warned the world against "the domino effect." He was afraid that
23 country after country was going to fall to soviet imperialism like dominoes. During
24 the Kennedy administration, the United States tried to take the control of Vietnam
25 away from the Soviets. The war continued into the Johnson administration. The
26 Vietnam War was a long, losing battle. It made many Americans wish to adopt a
27 more isolationist policy.

28 Since the collapse of the Soviet Union, the United States has been the world's
29 major superpower. It wants to remain in power fight terrorism promote peace and
30 do business all around the world. It looked like imperialism is here to stay.

1. What is the **best** change, if any, to make in the sentence in line 20 (*The United . . . War II.*)?

   a. Change *to* to **too**.
   b. Change *it's* to **its**.
   c. Change *win* to **winned**.
   d. Make no change.

2. The sentence in lines 29–30 (*It wants . . . the world.*) is poorly written. Which one of these is the **best** way to rewrite it?

   a. It wants to remains in power fight terrorism promote peace, and do business all around the world.
   b. It wants to remain in power, fight terrorism promote peace and do business all around the World.
   c. It wants to remain in power, fight terrorism, promote peace, and do business all around the world.
   d. It wants to promote fighting and power, terrorize business, and do it all over the world.

3. What is the **best** change, if any, to make in the sentence in line 4 (*We'll just . . . matters worse.*)?

   a. Change *make* to **made**.
   b. Insert quotation marks before **We'll**.
   c. Change the *period* to a **question mark**.
   d. Make no change.

4. What is the **best** change, if any, to make in the sentence in lines 22–23 (*He was . . . like dominoes.*)?

   a. Change *soviet* to **Soviet**.
   b. Change *imperialism* to **Imperialism**.
   c. Change *going* to **went**.
   d. Make no change.

5. Which transition would **best** fit at the beginning of the sentence in line 20 (*The United . . . War II.*)?

   a. However,
   b. Nevertheless,
   c. Amazingly,
   d. For example,

6. What is the **best** change, if any, to make in the sentence in lines 5–6 (*I know . . . your friend.*)?

   a. Insert quotation marks before **I**.
   b. Change *answers* to **Answers**.
   c. Insert a comma after **advice**.
   d. Make no change.

7. What is the **best** change, if any, to make in the sentence in lines 12–13 (*An isolationist . . . and prosperity.*)?

   a. Change *they're* to **there**.
   b. Change *be* to **have been**.
   c. Change *believes* to **beleives**.
   d. Make no change.

8. What is the **best** change, if any, to make in the sentence in line 30 (*It looked . . . to stay.*)?

   a. Change *to* to **two**.
   b. Change *looked* to **looks**.
   c. Insert a comma after **here**.
   d. Make no change.

9. What is the **best** change, if any, to make in the sentence in lines 9–10 (*Isolationist countries . . . or politics.*)?

   a. Change *too* to **to**.
   b. Insert a comma after **involved**.
   c. Change *countrie's* to **countries'**.
   d. Make no change.

10. What is the **best** change, if any, to make in the sentence in lines 10–12 (*They try . . . upon they.*)?

    a. Change *upon they* to **upon them**.
    b. Change *be* to **have been**.
    c. Change *depend* to **depends**.
    d. Make no change.

WHY ARE SOME PEOPLE ALLERGIC?

Kara's seventh-grade health class is studying allergies. Kara wanted to understand how an allergy works and why some people are allergic while others aren't. She went to the library and read about allergies. Then she took notes, organized them, and wrote a rough draft of a report about what causes allergies. She would like your help editing and revising it.

Here is Kara's rough draft. Read it and then answer questions 1–10.

1 Have you ever wondered why you seem to get poison ivy every single summer,
2 even if you stay out of the woods and don't go anywhere near a poison ivy plant? Do
3 you have a friend who can go hiking in the woods every day and has never even heard
4 of calamine lotion? When you are outside in the spring are you the one sneezing and
5 rubbing your itchy, watery eyes while your friend looks at you with pity?

6 Maybe you are like the lucky friend I just mentioned. Then again, maybe your
7 like me. I am an allergy sufferer, and now I understand more about why me am
8 allergic.

9 Scientists believe that we inherit the tendency to become allergic. This makes
10 sense since my mother and father both suffer from allergies, to. Scientists say that
11 a child has a greater chance of being allergic even if only one parent has allergies.
12 Allergies are triggered when the body is exposed to an "allergen." An allergen could
13 be a food, pollen, grass, a chemical, dust, dog hair, or one of many other things. In
14 people who have inherited allergies, allergens trigger nasty symptoms.

15 Scientists believe that even people whose parents are not allergic can sometimes
16 become allergic even if their parents are not allergic. A person could become allergic
17 if he or she is exposed to an allergen many times or for a prolonged period of time.

18 This is how an allergy works in the body. The immune system is supposed to fight
19 bad things that attack the body. When the body meets an invader, it makes special
20 proteins called "antibodies" that fight the enemy. The antibodies attach themselves
21 to tissues and to blood cells in the body, and they wait. When the invader comes
22 along, it fits into the antibody like a key fits into a lock. This tells the body's cells to
23 make chemicals that cause redness, swelling, itching, a runny nose, and other
24 symptoms.

25 An allergic reaction is sort of like a false alarm. The immune system gets messed
26 up and something like dog hair causes totally huge problems. That is why allergic
27 people get the symptoms of a cold when they are exposed to an allergen. Don't you
28 wish we could tell our overeager immune systems to just relax and enjoy the great
29 outdoors!

1. What is the **best** way to rewrite the sentence in lines 15–16 (*Scientists believe . . . not allergic.*) to improve the paragraph?

   a. Scientists believe that people whose parents are not allergic can become allergic no matter if their parents are allergic or not.
   b. Scientists believe that people whose parents are not allergic can sometimes become allergic themselves.
   c. Scientists believe that people can sometimes become allergic if their parents become allergic.
   d. Scientists believe that people become allergic, even if their parents have not become allergic, but even if they had.

2. What is the **best** change, if any, to make in the sentence in lines 27–29 (*Don't you . . . great outdoors!*)?

   a. Change the *exclamation point* to a **question mark**.
   b. Change *to* to **too**.
   c. Change *we* to **us**.
   d. Make no change.

3. What is the **best** change, if any, to make in the sentence in lines 6–7 (*Then again . . . like me.*)?

   a. Delete the comma after **again**.
   b. Change *me* to **I**.
   c. Change *your* to **you're**.
   d. Make no change.

4. What would be the **best** way to rewrite the sentence in lines 18–19 (*The immune . . . the body.*) to make it more specific?

   a. The immune system is supposed to fight bad things and other junk that attack the body.
   b. The immune system is supposed to fight harmful things like viruses and bacteria that attack the body.
   c. The immune system is supposed to fight stuff that attacks the body.
   d. The immune system is supposed to fight back against things attacking the body.

5. What is the **best** change, if any, to make in the sentence in lines 4–5 (*When you . . . with pity?*)?

   a. Change the *question mark* to a **period**.
   b. Insert a comma after **spring**.
   c. Change *your* to **you're**.
   d. Make no change.

6. What is the **best** change, if any, to make in the sentence in lines 9–10 (*This makes . . . allergies, to.*)?

   a. Change *mother and father* to **Mother and Father**.
   b. Insert a comma after **since**.
   c. Change *to* to **too**.
   d. Make no change.

7. Which of the following is the **best** supporting detail to add after the sentence in lines 16–17 (*A person . . . of time.*)?

   a. A person could become allergic if he or she is exposed to an allergen for a over an extended period.
   b. Allergies are a hassle.
   c. Scientists have been studying allergens.
   d. A florist who works in a flower shop every day might become allergic to roses, for example.

8. What is the **best** change, if any, to make in the sentence in lines 7–8 (*I am . . . am allergic.*)?

   a. Change *me* to **I**.
   b. Change *understand* to **understood**.
   c. Change *an* to **a**.
   d. Make no change.

9. Kara wants to add the following sentence to the third paragraph: *An allergen is anything that causes an allergic reaction in the body.* The sentence would **best** fit

   a. after the sentence in line 9 (*Scientists believe . . . become allergic.*).
   b. after the sentence in lines 10–11 (*Scientists say . . . has allergies.*).
   c. after the sentence in line 12 (*Allergies are . . . an "allergen."*).
   d. after the sentence in lines 13–14 (*In people . . . nasty symtoms.*).

10. Instead of the sentence in lines 25–26 (*The immune . . . huge problems.*), which of these uses the **best** tone for this audience?

    a. The immune system gets messes up and dog hair is a big issue.
    b. The immune system encounters big problems from dog hairs and other junk.
    c. The immune system can't handle all the crazy allergens in the air, even something like dog hair.
    d. The immune system malfunctions and treats a harmless allergen, such as dog hair, like an enemy invader.

Origins of Astrology

Lynn's seventh-grade history class is studying Alexander the Great. Her teacher asks each student to choose a topic somehow relating to Alexander the Great and his conquests and to write a report on it. Lynn has written her outline and rough draft. She needs your help editing and revising it.

Here is Lynn's rough draft. Read it and then answer questions 1–10.

1 Thousands of years ago, astrology was only for members of royalty. An astrologer
2 could look forward to a comfortable life if he or she was well liked. If the court
3 astrologer's news made the royal benefactor angry, the astrologer would most likely
4 lose his or her head.

5 Western Tropical astronomy dates from ancient Mesopotamia around 2300 B.C.E.
6 It made it's way to ancient Greece in about 600 B.C.E. In fact, the first astrologers
7 appeared in Greece with the first philosophers, men such as Socrates, Plato, and
8 Aristotle. Alexander the Great was a student of Aristotle. Therefore, between 336
9 B.C.E. and 323 B.C.E., he spread Greek culture and thought over a much wider area
10 as he conquered other lands.

11 From 323 B.C.E. to 31 B.C.E., Alexandria Egypt, became the center of Greek
12 thought and philosophy. During this time, astrology did well among important
13 thinkers of this time. Horoscopes, zodiac signs, and individual astrological readings
14 appeared. Astrology was no longer just for royalty.

15 During the Middle Ages, the popularity of astrology began to fade in the Western
16 world. It made a comeback during the European Renaissance, which lasted in some
17 places until the 1670s. Men such as Marsilio Ficino were practicing Catholics,
18 astrologers, and philosophers. Scientists figured out in the seventeenth century that
19 Earth was not the center of the universe, astrology suffered a terrible blow.
20 Meanwhile, astronomy became more important.

21 Less than two hundred years ago, astrology in Western society gained in
22 popularity once again. Astrologers Sepharial (1860–1917) and Alan Leo (1864–1929)
23 were fascinating, energetic, and mysterious. They drew peoples' interest and
24 founded the Theosophical Society in Great Britain. In the twentieth century, ideas
25 like karma, reincarnation, and daily horoscopes became extremely popular.
26 Astrologer Paul Clancy's magazine, *American Astrology* became a huge success in
27 1934. *American Astrology*'s reputation is believed to have sparked people's interest
28 in daily and weekly astrological columns. They commonly appear in newspapers and
29 magazines in the United States today. They also show up in newspapers and
30 magazines in Great Britain.

1. The sentence in lines 8–10 (*Therefore, between . . . other lands.*) is poorly written. Which one of these is the **best** way to rewrite it?

    a. Greek culture and thought were spread over other lands between 336 B.C.E. and 323 B.C.E. since Alexander the Great was Greek.
    b. Therefore, he spread Greek culture and thought over a much wider area as he conquered other lands between 336 B.C.E. and 323 B.C.E., since he was a student of Aristotle.
    c. Between 336 B.C.E. and 323 B.C.E., Alexander's conquest of other lands spread Greek culture and thought over a much wider area.
    d. By conquering other lands between 336 B.C.E. and 323 B.C.E., he spread Greek culture and thought over a much wider area.

2. Which transition would **best** fit at the beginning of the sentence in lines 2–4 (*If the . . . her head.*)?

    a. However,
    b. For example,
    c. Therefore,
    d. Consequently,

3. What is the **best** change, if any, to make in the sentence in lines 23–24 (*They drew . . . Great Britain.*)?

    a. Change *Theosophical Society* to **theosophical society**.
    b. Change *peoples'* to **people's**.
    c. Change *drew* to **drawed**.
    d. Make no change.

4. What is the **best** change, if any, to make in the sentence in lines 6–8 (*In fact . . . and Aristotle.*)?

    a. Change *philosophers* to **Philosophers**.
    b. Insert a comma after **Greece**.
    c. Delete the comma after **Socrates**.
    d. Make no change.

5. What is the **best** way to rewrite the sentence in lines 12–13 (*During this . . . this time.*) to improve the paragraph?

    a. During this time, astrology did good among important thinkers of this time.
    b. During this time, astrology did well among important thinkers.
    c. During this time, important thinkers did well with astrology.
    d. During this time, astrology was good and well among important thinkers of this time.

6. What is the **best** change, if any, to make in the sentence in line 6 (*It made . . . 600 B.C.E.*)?

    a. Change *it's* to **its**.
    b. Change *ancient* to **Ancient**.
    c. Change *to* to **too**.
    d. Make no change.

7. The sentence in lines 18–19 (*Scientists figured . . . terrible blow.*) is poorly written. Which one of these is the **best** way to rewrite it?

    a. Scientists, in the seventeenth century, knew that Earth was not the center of the Universe, so astrology suffered a terrible blow.
    b. In the seventeenth century, scientists figured out that Earth was not the center of the universe, astrology suffered a terrible blow.
    c. Astrology suffered a terrible blow when scientists figured out that earth was not the center of the Universe in the seventeenth century.
    d. When scientists figured out in the seventeenth century that Earth was not the center of the universe, astrology suffered a terrible blow.

8. What is the **best** change, if any, to make in the sentence in lines 11–12 (*From 323 . . . and philosophy.*)?

    a. Change *became* to **become**.
    b. Delete the comma after **B.C.E.**
    c. Insert a comma after **Alexandria**.
    d. Make no change.

9. Which of the following is the **best** way to combine the two sentences in lines 28–30 (*They commonly . . . Great Britain.*)?

   a. Great Britain's newspapers and magazines commonly have them and so do the United States'.
   b. The United States and Great Britain both appear in newspapers and magazines today.
   c. The United States' newspapers and magazines commonly feature them as well as do Great Britain's newspapers and magazines.
   d. Today, they commonly appear in newspapers and magazines in both the United States and Great Britain.

10. What is the **best** change, if any, to make in the sentence in lines 26–27 (*Astrologer Paul . . . in 1934.*)?

    a. Change *Clancy's* to **Clancys'**.
    b. Insert a comma after **Astrology**.
    c. Delete the comma after **magazine**.
    d. Make no change.

ANGER MANAGEMENT

Hector's seventh-grade social studies class is doing a unit on health and the emotions. He has been asked to write an imaginary letter to a friend who has been showing an emotional behavior and describe how this behavior is affecting the friend's life. Hector chooses to write about anger. He does some research, writes an ouline, and constructs his rough draft. He needs your help editing and revising it.

Here is Hector's rough draft. Read it and then answer questions 1–10.

1   Dear Chloe

2   I am writing this letter to you because I have noticed that you have been acting
3   particularly angry over the past few weeks. I think I can help you to better
4   understand the source of your anger and how to manage it.

5   Anger is a normal, healthy human emotion. Unless it gets out of control. It can
6   lead to problems at home, at school, and with your friends. It can also make you feel
7   like you don't have control over your life. Sometimes, I think you feel this way. Anger
8   causes a person's heart rate and blood pressure rates to go up. His or her adrenaline
9   and hormone levels increase as well.

10   You may not even be clear as to why your so upset all the time. It could be that
11 you're angry with a specific person, like a friend, family member, or teacher. You
12 could be mad about an event, such as failing a test or missing the bus. Also,
13 memories of trauma can cause anger.

14   Many times, people use aggression to express their anger. However, you can't lash
15 out at every person or thing, that makes you mad or annoys you. Laws, society, and
16 common sense will tell you that. There are a few ways that you can manage your
17 anger to kept a better handle on it in the future.

18   Expressing your angry feelings in a non-aggressive, assertive way is the
19 healthiest way to relieve yourself of the emotion. You must learn to communicate
20 your needs to others in a clear, positive, respectful way. Some people use the second
21 technique: suppression. The goal is to convert the anger into constructive behavior.
22 However, suppression often leads to tense, depressed feelings, and high blood
23 pressure. The third way to control your anger is to calm down inside. By controlling
24 your external and internal responses and taking steps to lower your heart rate, the
25 feelings will generally decrease.

26   Unexpressed anger can cause many problems. People who constantly put others
27 down, criticize everything, and make cynical comments haven't learned how to
28 express their anger constructively. Unfortunately, they seldom have positive
29 relationships with others. You can be a real jerk sometimes, so I wanted to tell you
30 this right away.

(continued on next page)

(continued from previous page)

```
31      The best step you can take is to identify what makes you angry and than develop
32   strategies to keep you from going over the edge.  Life is filled with frustration, loss,
33   pain, and unpredictability.  By changing the way events and people affect you—
34   thereby minimizing angry and frustrated reactions—you'll enjoy a much happier life.

35                              sincerely yours,

36                                      Hector
```

1. What is the **best** change, if any, to make in the phrase in line 35 (*sincerely yours,*)?

    a. Change the *comma* to a **period**.
    b. Change *sincerely* to **Sincerely**.
    c. Change *sincerely* to **sinseerly**.
    d. Make no change.

2. Hector wants to add the following sentence to the fifth paragraph in the body of the letter: *If you hold in your anger, stop thinking about it, and focus on something positive, you are using suppression.* The sentence would **best** fit

    a. after the sentence in lines 19–20 (*You must . . . respectful way.*).
    b. after the sentence in lines 20–21 (*Some people . . . technique: suppression.*).
    c. after the sentence in lines 22–23 (*However, suppression . . . blood pressure.*).
    d. after the sentence in line 23 (*The third . . . down inside.*).

3. What is the **best** change, if any, to make in the sentence in line 10 (*You may . . . the time.*)?

    a. Change *your* to **you're**.
    b. Change *upset* to **upsetted**.
    c. Insert a comma after **clear**.
    d. Make no change.

4. Where is there an incomplete sentence?

    a. in lines 28–29 (*Unfortunately, they . . . with others.*)
    b. in lines 15–16 (*Laws, society . . . you that.*)
    c. in line 5 (*Unless it . . . of control.*)
    d. in lines 33–34 (*By changing . . . happier life.*)

5. What is the **best** change, if any, to make in the sentence in lines 14–15 (*However, you . . . annoys you.*)?

   a. Insert a comma after **mad**.
   b. Change *lash* to **lashes**.
   c. Delete the comma after **thing**.
   d. Make no change.

6. What is the **best** change, if any, to make in the phrase in line 1 (*Dear Chloe*)?

   a. Insert a period after **Chloe**.
   b. Insert a comma after **Chloe**.
   c. Change *Dear* to **Deer**.
   d. Make no change.

7. Instead of the sentence in lines 29–30 (*You can . . . right away.*), which of these uses the **best** tone for this audience?

   a. It's not like I care, but it would be really annoying if you got like that.
   b. You have a tendency to be really irritating and bad-tempered, so listen up.
   c. I wanted to inform you of your problem right away, so you wouldn't waste any more time being mean to everybody.
   d. I don't want to see that happen to you.

8. What is the **best** change, if any, to make in the sentence in lines 31–32 (*The best . . . the edge.*)?

   a. Change *than* to **then**.
   b. Change *strategies* to **strageties**.
   c. Change *going* to **gone**.
   d. Make no change.

9. What is the **best** change, if any, to make in the sentence in lines 16–17 (*There are . . . the future.*)?

   a. Insert a comma after **ways**.
   b. Change *your* to **you're**.
   c. Change *kept* to **keep**.
   d. Make no change.

10. Which of the following is the **best** supporting detail to add after the sentence in lines 31–32 (*The best . . . the edge.*)?

    a. If you're feeling sad and lonely, just get angry and you'll feel better.
    b. If you need to talk to someone about it, go to an adult who seems really mad all the time, so they can understand that there are other people out there like them.
    c. Follow a set plan to find your way to happiness, such as getting really mad and breaking stuff that belongs to your friends.
    d. Change the way you think, use silliness and laughter to brighten a tense moment, or give yourself a break from the situation or environment that is triggering your anger.

Peer Tutoring

Eric's seventh-grade social studies teacher has requested that each student write a report expressing his or her opinion on the following question: *If you were having difficulty with a certain subject in school, do you think you would learn better from one of your peers or from an adult instructor?* Eric made a web of ideas for and against peer tutoring and wrote his report. He needs your help editing and revising it.

Here is Eric's rough draft. Read it and then answer questions 1–10.

1 If I was having trouble in a certain subject, I think it would be usefuller to get help
2 from someone my age. In researching this topic, I learned that students gain many
3 helpful skills through peer tutoring. Tutoring benefits both the tutor and the other
4 student (the tutee).

5 I've learned that students become stronger in academics. Meanwhile, there social
6 behaviors, classroom discipline, and relationships improve as well. Plus, peer
7 tutoring could led more students to want to enter teaching later on in life. The skills
8 learned in peer tutoring could also turn into good parenting skills.

9 Peer tutoring in math and language arts bennefits both the tutor and the tutee.
10 Mostly, the tutors gain further skills in understanding the subject matter. Tutees
11 earn higher grades in the subjects, while better understanding the subject as a whole.
12 I'm pretty good at math.

13 One reason peer tutoring is so effective is because kids all speak the same
14 language. The tutee feels like he or she is on the same level as the tutor. The tutee
15 is more likely to do certain things in front of another student. Communication
16 between the two students is probably more casual and more balanced. Therefore, the
17 fact that the tutor is in a position of higher status doesn't mean as much in peer
18 tutoring.

19 Those students working as tutors have to be trained in how to do it correctly. No
20 matter what their academic skills, they must understand that they have a
21 responsibility to the students working under they as tutees. Teachers must be
22 involved in this process. Therefore, peer tutoring still involves adult supervision.
23 Tutors will form a better relationship with the student they're tutoring, who learn to
24 be responsible, capable models for their tutees.

25 Tutees gain a firmer understanding of the subject they am struggling with.
26 Tutoring teaches about fairness and improves self-esteem. It makes kids more
27 willing to share and be kind to others. Peer tutoring boosts communication and
28 develops creative and critical thinking skills.

29 Through the research I've done, I've learned that peer tutoring could be good. I
30 feel that it would be more rewarding and fun to be tutored by someone with whom I
31 have more in common.

1. What would be the **best** way to rewrite the sentence in lines 14–15 (*The tutee . . . another student.*) to make it more specific?

    a. The tutee is more likely to speak freely in front of another student.
    b. The tutee is more likely to feel at ease in front of another student.
    c. The tutee is more likely to relax in front of another student.
    d. The tutee is more likely to ask questions, give opinions, and risk guessing the wrong answer in front of another student.

2. What is the **best** change, if any, to make in the sentence in lines 1–2 (*If I . . . my age.*)?

    a. Change *usefuller* to **more useful**.
    b. Delete the comma after **subject**.
    c. Change *having* to **had**.
    d. Make no change.

3. What is the **best** change, if any, to make in the sentence in lines 6–7 (*Plus, peer . . . in life.*)?

    a. Change *to enter* to **entering**.
    b. Insert a comma after **tutoring**.
    c. Change *led* to **lead**.
    d. Make no change.

4. Which one of these sentences does **not** belong?

    a. the sentence in lines 16–18 (*Therefore, the . . . peer tutoring.*)
    b. the sentence in lines 29–31 (*I feel . . . in common.*)
    c. the sentence in line 12 (*I'm pretty . . . at math.*)
    d. the sentence in line 22 (*Therefore, peer . . . adult supervision.*)

5. What is the **best** change, if any, to make in the sentence in lines 5–6 (*Meanwhile, there . . . as well.*)?

    a. Change *well* to **good**.
    b. Change *there* to **their**.
    c. Delete the comma after **behaviors**.
    d. Make no change.

6. What is the **best** change, if any, to make in the sentence in lines 19–21 (*No matter . . . as tutees.*)?

   a. Change *their* to **they're**.
   b. Change *under they* to **under them**.
   c. Change the *period* to a **question mark**.
   d. Make no change.

7. The sentence in lines 23–24 (*Tutors will . . . their tutees.*) is poorly written. Which one of these is the **best** way to rewrite it?

   a. Tutors who learn to be responsible, capable models for their tutees will form a better relationship with them.
   b. Tutors will form a better relationship with their tutees if they form a better relationship.
   c. Tutors and tutees will have a better relationship if they learn to be responsible, capable models for each other.
   d. Tutors will learn to be responsible, capable models while they are forming a better relationship with their tutees.

8. What is the **best** change, if any, to make in the sentence in line 9 (*Peer tutoring . . . the tutee.*)?

   a. Change the *period* to a **comma**.
   b. Change *bennefitted* to **benefited**.
   c. Change *tutoring* to **tutor**.
   d. Make no change.

9. What is the **best** change, if any, to make in the sentence in line 25 (*Tutees gain . . . struggling with.*)?

   a. Change *firmer* to **more firmer**.
   b. Insert a comma after **subject**.
   c. Change *am* to **are**.
   d. Make no change.

10. The sentence in line 29 (*Through the . . . be good.*) is poorly written. Which one of these is the **best** way to rewrite it?

    a. Peer tutoring is good, and I know that because I've done a lot of research.
    b. Through the research I've done, I learned that peer tutoring can work out pretty well.
    c. I've done a lot of research and have come to the conclusion that peer tutoring could be good because I've done research on that.
    d. Through the research I've done, I've learned the many benefits of peer tutoring.

Film Critic

Josephine's school had a Career Day for the seventh grade. Following this special event, each student was asked to submit a short report describing the career he or she had found most interesting. Josephine liked the presentation about becoming a film critic the most, so she outlined her ideas and wrote a rough draft on that subject. She needs your help editing and revising it.

Here is Josephine's rough draft. Read it and then answer questions 1–10.

1 I found the film criticism segment of today's Career Day to be the most
2 fascinating. The best thing about being a film critic is that anyone who loves movies
3 can enjoy doing it. Ellen Simmons seemed to get a lot out of her work, who gave the
4 talk on being a film critic. She said that she never dreaded sitting down to watch a
5 movie, so why shouldn't she enjoy being a film critic! I have to say that it sounds
6 pretty good to me.

7 Mrs. Simmons recommends that a student wanting to work as a film critic for a
8 newspaper should become a journalist first. In the meantime, the person should
9 continuously write about film whenever he or she can. She also thinks that watching
10 movies on the "big screen" gave her a much better perspective on the films she were
11 seeing. Watching movies at home didn't seem to be quite as effective at giving her
12 an impression of the movie.

13 Once you become a film critic, Mrs. Simmons says that the best way to critique a
14 film is by staying objective. She doesn't pay attention to the stars cast in the movie
15 or the director or the stars that are in it. She rarely listens to other people's opinions
16 on the film. She focuses her complete attention on the movie itself.

17 Some students asked Mrs. Simmons, if she thought writing in the first person
18 (using "I") in film criticisms was a wise idea. Mrs. Simmons felt that writing in the
19 first person was perfectly acceptable and maybe even more enjoyable reading. Since
20 the writer could display a bit more personality as he or she wrote. She warned,
21 however, that writing criticisms in first person left the writer open to personal
22 attacks from displeased readers. He or she could expect very favorable responses
23 from readers who agreed with the criticism.

24 A common trick used to show that you are knowledgeable about movies of all
25 kinds and from all times is to compare films from the past to the movie you are
26 currently critiquing. Mrs. Simmons recommends including these comparisons
27 frequently in writing. However, if you do not possess this kind of knowledge of movie
28 history, don't fake it. You're wiser readers will know.

29 Film critics write to many audiences. Their work is often in college newspapers,
30 daily, weekly, or monthly publications, and on websites. No matter who is in your
31 audience, you want to write clearly. You never know who may be reading your piece.

32 Mrs. Simmons not only got me exited about being a film critic. She also made me
33 want to write a film criticism column for our school newspaper!

1. What is the **best** change, if any, to make in the sentence in line 32 (*Mrs. Simmons . . . film critic.*)?

    a. Change *me* to **I**.
    b. Change the *period* to a **question mark**.
    c. Change *exited* to **excited**.
    d. Make no change.

2. The sentence in lines 3–4 (*Ellen Simmons . . . film critic.*) is poorly written. Which one of these is the **best** way to rewrite it?

    a. Ellen Simmons, who gave the talk on being a film critic, seemed to get a lot out of her work.
    b. Ellen Simmons seemed to get a lot out of the talk on being a film critic.
    c. Ellen Simmons's film critic gave a talk and seemed to get a lot out of her work.
    d. Ellen Simmons's work as a film critic gave a talk on being a film critic and her work.

3. What is the **best** way to rewrite the sentence in lines 14–15 (*She doesn't . . . in it.*) to improve the paragraph?

    a. She doesn't pay attention to neither the stars cast in the movie nor the director.
    b. She doesn't pay attention to the director, the stars cast in the movie, or the stars in the movie.
    c. She doesn't pay attention to the stars cast in the movie, the movie, or the director.
    d. She doesn't pay attention to the stars cast in the movie or to the director.

4. What is the **best** change, if any, to make in the sentence in lines 9–11 (*She also . . . were seeing.*)?

    a. Change *watching* to **watched**.
    b. Change *were* to **was**.
    c. Insert quotation marks after **seeing.**
    d. Make no change.

5. What is the **best** change, if any, to make in the sentence in lines 4–5 (*She said . . . film critic!*)?

   a. Change the *exclamation point* to a **question mark**.
   b. Delete the comma after **movie**.
   c. Change *dreaded* to **dredded**.
   d. Make no change.

6. Where is there an incomplete sentence?

   a. in line 28 (*You're wiser . . . will know.*)
   b. in lines 5–6 (*I have . . . to me.*)
   c. in lines 19–20 (*Since the . . . she wrote.*)
   d. in lines 30–31 (*No matter . . . write clearly.*)

7. What is the **best** change, if any, to make in the sentence in lines 17–18 (*Some students . . . wise idea.*)?

   a. Change *writing* to **wrote**.
   b. Delete the comma after **Simmons**.
   c. Change the *parentheses* to **quotation marks**.
   d. Make no change.

8. The sentence in lines 11–12 (*Watching movies . . . the movie.*) is poorly written. Which one of these is the **best** way to rewrite it?

   a. Watching movies at home, as effective as it was at giving her an impression of the movie, didn't seem to be as effective.
   b. Watching movies at home did not leave her with as effectively impressed upon the movie.
   c. Watching movies at home, on the other hand, didn't seem to be quite as effective.
   d. Effectively impressed with movies as she was, watching them at home just didn't do it quite as well.

9. What is the **best** change, if any, to make in the sentence in line 28 (*You're wiser . . . will know.*)?

    a. Change *wiser* to **wizer**.
    b. Change *You're* to **Your**.
    c. Change the *period* to a **question mark**.
    d. Make no change.

10. Which transition would **best** fit at the beginning of the sentence in lines 22–23 (*He or . . . the criticism.*)?

    a. On the other hand,
    b. Fortunately,
    c. For instance,
    d. Amazingly,

Advertisers Lure Teens

Christian's social studies class has been studying social pressures. His teacher has asked that each student write a persuasive report on something in contemporary society that influences teenagers. Christian visits his library, writes an outline, and writes his report. He needs your help editing and revising it.

Here is Christian's rough draft. Read it and then answer questions 1–10.

1 Advertising is a powerful form of communication. Without even realizing it, an
2 average American sees over 5,000 advertisements every day. Advertisers in the
3 United States must keep up with the trends and interests of the entire population.
4 What they have learned over time, however, is the incredible buying power of the
5 teenage consumer. Is advertising just a means of selling a product, or is it a way to
6 manipulate people as well.

7 Advertisers do their research. They watch what we do, what we're interested in,
8 and what we hope one day to be. By conducting surveys on the phone and written
9 questionnaires and offering samples of their products advertisers get an idea of how
10 the average American reacts to what is being sold. These kinds of research is
11 necessary in advertising. However, not all the methods advertisers employ are
12 moral.

13 Advertisers commonly use people's fears and insecurities to get them to buy
14 products. Pharmaceutical company's television ads, for example, could lead people to
15 believe that they need the advertised drugs. In fact, those people could be in perfect
16 health.

17 Teenagers are the top consumers in today's society, so many advertisers have
18 shifted their focus to target them. Many teenagers have part-time jobs and do not
19 have bills to pay. Therefore, their money is mainly spent on leisure activities, such
20 as shopping and going to the movies. Advertisers may also enjoy these activities.

21 Teenagers are constantly changing and the advertising industry tries to change
22 with them. Most teenagers want to be individuals. At the same time, they don't want
23 to be too separate from the group. They usually have this "life is good" attitude and
24 then spend their money without using their brains. Keeping up with changing
25 trends is also important to many teenagers, which leads advertisers to pitch to them
26 even more aggressively. Advertisers will make original, flashy, and funny ads to
27 appeal to teenagers. They will use popular music and dancing. Not too long ago, the
28 Gap became the most fashionable clothing store because of the popularity of their
29 swing music commercials.

30 Celebrities often appeal to teenagers. Therefore, advertisers create ads and
31 brands endorsed by celebrities. People are often mistakenly led to believe that
32 certain products will bringing about popularity and happiness. Nike ads, for
33 example, often portray star athletes wearing the nike brand. Is it the shoes that
34 made the athlete popular? Certainly not.

(continued on next page)

(continued from previous page)

> 35   The advertising industry can be harmful to teenagers. It teaches impulsive
> 36 spending habits. It also teaches that popularity and fitting in are more important
> 37 than individuality. Advertising may be misleading and in some cases immoral.
> 38 Nevertheless, consumers must learn to make intelligent buying decisions.

1. What is the **best** change, if any, to make in the sentence in lines 32–33 (*Nike ads . . . nike brand.*)?

    a. Change *athletes* to **athleets**.
    b. Change *nike* to **Nike**.
    c. Delete the comma after **example**.
    d. Make no change.

2. Which one of these sentences does **not** belong?

    a. the sentence in lines 33–34 (*Is it . . . athlete popular?*)
    b. the sentence in lines 10–11 (*These kinds . . . in advertising.*)
    c. the sentence in lines 2–3 (*Advertisers in . . . entire population.*)
    d. the sentence in line 20 (*Advertisers may . . . these activities.*)

3. Instead of the sentence in lines 23–24 (*They usually . . . their brains.*), which of these uses the **best** tone for this audience?

    a. They spend their money all over the place and then wonder why everything is so great all the time.
    b. They're like, "Hey, everything's cool. Let's go buy new stuff."
    c. They are often optimistic and like to impulsively buy new things.
    d. They have a good attitude, which leads them to think that spending their money is a bad idea.

4. What is the **best** change, if any, to make in the sentence in lines 5–6 (*Is advertising . . . as well.*)?

    a. Change the *period* to a **question mark**.
    b. Change *it* to **them**.
    c. Change *well* to **good**.
    d. Make no change.

5. What is the **best** change, if any, to make in the sentence in lines 14–15 (*Pharmaceutical company's ... advertised drugs.*)?

    a. Change *ads* to **adds**.
    b. Change *company's* to **companies'**.
    c. Change *they* to **them**.
    d. Make no change.

6. What is the **best** change, if any, to make in the sentence in lines 31–32 (*People are ... and happiness.*)?

    a. Change *bringing* to **bring**.
    b. Change *led* to **lead**.
    c. Change *are* to **is**.
    d. Make no change.

7. The sentence in lines 8–10 (*By conducting ... being sold.*) is poorly written. Which one of these is the **best** way to rewrite it?

    a. Conducting surveys over the phone and written questionnaires over the phone and offering samples over the phone will let advertisers get an idea of how the average American reacts to what is being sold.
    b. With phones, questionnaires, and samples, advertisers will get an idea of how the average American reacts to what is being sold.
    c. Conducting surveys on the phone and written questionnaires, offering samples of their products, advertisers get an idea of how the average American reacts to what is being sold.
    d. By conducting phone surveys, taking written questionnaires, and offering samples of their products, advertisers get an idea of how the average American reacts to what is being sold.

8. What is the **best** change, if any, to make in the sentence in lines 21–22 (*Teenagers are ... with them.*)?

    a. Change *industry* to **industree**.
    b. Change *allows* to **allowed**.
    c. Insert a comma after **changing**.
    d. Make no change.

9. What is the **best** change, if any, to make in the sentence in lines 10–11 (*These kinds . . . in advertising.*)?

   a. Change *research* to **researchs**.
   b. Change *is* to **are**.
   c. Change *kinds* to **kinds'**.
   d. Make no change.

10. The sentence in lines 24–26 (*Keeping up . . . more aggressively.*) is poorly written. Which one of these is the **best** way to rewrite it?

    a. Because many teenagers try to keep up with changing trends, advertisers will pitch to them even more aggressively.
    b. Thinking that keeping up with trends is important, teenagers and advertisers pitch to them even more aggressively.
    c. Keeping up with changing trends is also important to teenagers so that advertisers will pitch to them even more aggressively.
    d. Aggressively pitching to teenagers to keep up with changing trends will make teenagers pitch them.

SNOWBOARDING   33

Kynara's seventh-grade history class is writing reports about topics relating to twentieth-century United States' history. Kynara chooses to write about the history of snowboarding. She composes an outline and writes her rough draft. She needs your help editing and revising it.

Here is Kynara's rough draft. Read it and then answer questions 1–10.

1   Skiing has been around in the United States since the early twentieth century.
2   Since that time, the retail industry dealing in Winter sports has steadily grown. In
3   the 1990s, it skyrocketed. For the first time in history, snowboarding was the cause.

4   Snowboarding first appeared in 1972. A fifteen-year-old kid named Jake Burton
5   decided that he was bored with skiing and wanted to try something new. He built his
6   first snowboard in about three weeks. Burton take his new invention to the nearby
7   ski slopes to test it out. Unfortunately, he was denied access time and time again.
8   Burton didn't need a professional ski slope to practice on his prototype snowboard,
9   however. He continued to try to gain access to ski slopes, but had no luck. He realized
10 that the only way to prove what his invention could do was to make a video of himself
11 riding it.

12 Burton met Craig Kelly shortly thereafter. When he heard about Burton's idea,
13 Kelly enthusiastically offered to produce his video. In the meantime, Burton had
14 produced several more snowboards that his closest friends had been riding. Burton
15 and Kelly took they're video to the ski slopes and showed it around. They finally met
16 with success at Okemo, whose management agreed to allow Burton to ride during the
17 week. Burton snowboards, inc., was born.

18 In the 1980s, the growth of snowboarding was slow and many ski slopes still
19 would not allow snowboarders on their trails. In the 1990s, Generation X made many
20 things popular. Snowboarding rapidly became the next big thing in winter sports.
21 By 1991, as many as 85 percent of all ski resorts allowed snowboarders to share the
22 slopes with skiers.

23 Soon, problems arose between skiers and snowboarders. There were more
24 accidents as snowboarders practicing their tricks on the slopes—and often fall down
25 trying—got in the way of skiers simply making their way down the mountain. Parks
26 designed exclusively for snowboarders began popping up across the country.

27 Snowboarding brought with it an new, original image. Snowboarders dressed
28 differently and had different hairstyles. The theme of the 1990s was being different.
29 Snowboarding fit right in. It wasn't just the resort industry that was capitalizing on
30 the new sport. Retail outlets were also greatly benefiting from the new business.
31 Snowboarding equipment was often cheaper than ski equipment, so many younger
32 people could afford it. Snowboarding lessons became another profitable business.

33 Snowboarding seems to only be gaining in popularity. It brings with a fresh,
34 independent spirit that almost anyone can enjoy.

1. What would be the **best** way to rewrite the sentence in lines 19–20 (*In the . . . things popular.*) to make it more specific?

    a. In the 1990s, Generation X made lots of stuff popular.
    b. In the 1990s, Generation X made skateboarding, BMX bikes, bungee jumping, and rollerblading popular.
    c. In the 1990s, Generation X liked many things that then became popular.
    d. In the 1990s, Generation X found a ton of activities that made them happy.

2. What is the **best** change, if any, to make in the sentence in line 17 (*Burton snowboards . . . was born.*)?

    a. Change *was* to **were**.
    b. Delete the comma after **snowboards**.
    c. Change *snowboards, inc.* to **Snowboards, Inc.**
    d. Make no change.

3. What is the **best** change, if any, to make in the sentence in lines 6–7 (*Burton take . . . it out.*)?

    a. Change *new* to **knew**.
    b. Change *to* to **two**.
    c. Change *take* to **took**.
    d. Make no change.

4. What is the **best** change, if any, to make in the sentence in lines 31–32 (*Snowboarding equipment . . . afford it.*)?

    a. Change *than* to **then**.
    b. Delete the comma after **equipment**.
    c. Change *more younger* to **youngerer**.
    d. Make no change.

5. What is the **best** change, if any, to make in the sentence in line 2 (*Since that . . . steadily grown.*)?

    a. Change *grown* to **growed**.
    b. Change *Winter* to **winter**.
    c. Delete the comma after **time**.
    d. Make no change.

6. Which of the following is the **best** supporting detail to add after the sentence in line 12 (*Burton met . . . shortly thereafter.*)?

   a. Kelly was already filming skateboarding and skiing videos.
   b. Burton was fifteen years old in 1972.
   c. Even then, snowboarding was still fairly knew.
   d. Skiing was still popular at this time.

7. What is the **best** change, if any, to make in the sentence in line 27 (*Snowboarding brought . . . original image.*)?

   a. Change *an* to **a**.
   b. Change *image* to **images**.
   c. Insert a comma after **original**.
   d. Make no change.

8. Kynara wants to add the following sentence to the second paragraph: *He trekked along backcountry trails instead to learn what the snowboard could do.* This sentence would **best** fit

   a. after the sentence in line 4 (*Snowboarding first . . . in 1972.*).
   b. after the sentence in lines 5–6 (*He built . . . three weeks.*).
   c. after the sentence in line 7 (*Unfortunately, he . . . time again.*).
   d. after the sentence in lines 8–9 (*Burton didn't . . . snowboard, however.*).

9. What is the **best** change, if any, to make in the sentence in lines 23–25 (*There were . . . the mountain.*)?

   a. Change *their tricks* to **there tricks**.
   b. Change *fall* to **falling**.
   c. Insert a comma after **skiers**.
   d. Make no change.

10. What is the **best** change, if any, to make in the sentence in lines 14–15 (*Burton and . . . it around.*)?

    a. Change *took* to **had taken**.
    b. Change *to* to **too**.
    c. Change *they're* to **their**.
    d. Make no change.

EATING DISORDERS IN MEN? 34

The seventh-grade class has been learning about health. Each student has been asked to write a report about a specific health issue. Pete does some research at the local library, makes a web of ideas, and writes his rough draft. He needs your help editing and revising it.

Here is Pete's rough draft. Read it and then answer questions 1–10.

1   Eating disorders have been a common issue in women's health. Women aren't the
2   only ones unhappy with their looks, however. Some of these same disorders now
3   affect men in the United States, such as anorexia nervosa and bulimia. In fact, as
4   many as one million men suffer from eating disorders.

5   Many males may think that they are compulsive eaters. They may actually have
6   a binge eating disorder like bulimia. "Bulimia" involves rapidly eating lots of food
7   and than vomiting it up to prevent weight gain. Sufferers of "anorexia nervosa," on
8   the other hand, stop eating because they are afraid of gaining weight. Symptoms of
9   this disorder include nervousness combined with lose of appetite.

10 Males with these disorders tend to be more active. They are also usually anxious
11 about food, and weight. Teasing can lead a man to develop an eating disorder. He
12 may also fear weight-related illnesses found in other family members or want to
13 remove extra flab from part of his body. Both men and women with eating disorders
14 want to look like people in magazines. Men with careers in modeling or acting
15 commonly have them. A man with an eating disorder may also desire to be a better
16 athlete. Men suffering from bulimia and anorexia nervosa are often involved in
17 sports that stress dieting. Body builders are at high risk.

18 Unfortunately, many men are unwilling to confess their problems. In fact, many
19 health professionals don't expect to see men with eating disorders. They may
20 misdiagnose men suffering from bulimia or anorexia. Since eating disorder
21 treatment programs were designed mainly for women. Men may feel uncomfortable
22 in that environment. If a man can commit to a well-run, effective program he will
23 most likely recover successfully.

24 The American public seems preoccupies with weight loss nowadays. It is no
25 wonder that eating disorders are becoming more common in both men and women.
26 As long as these societal pressures exist, we can expect the number of cases to
27 continue to rise. Researchers are still learning how best to diagnose and treat men
28 with these diseases.

1. Which transition would **best** fit at the beginning of the sentence in lines 19–20 (*They may . . . or anorexia.*)?

    a. For example,
    b. Therefore,
    c. In fact,
    d. However,

2. What is the **best** change, if any, to make in the sentence in lines 6–7 (*"Bulimia" involves . . . weight gain.*)?

    a. Change *weight* to **wayt**.
    b. Change *than* to **then**.
    c. Insert a comma after **up**.
    d. Make no change.

3. Where is there an incomplete sentence?

    a. in lines 8–9 (*Symptoms of . . . of appetite.*)
    b. in lines 3–4 (*In fact . . . eating disorders.*)
    c. in lines 27–28 (*Researchers are . . . these diseases.*)
    d. in lines 20–21 (*Since eating . . . for women.*)

4. The sentence in lines 2–3 (*Some of . . . and bulimia.*) is poorly written. Which one of these is the **best** way to rewrite it?

    a. Some of these same disorders—such as anorexia nervosa and bulimia—now affect men in the United States.
    b. Such as anorexia nervosa and bulimia, some of these same disorders now affect men in the United States.
    c. In the United States, some of these same disorders now affect men in the United States.
    d. Some of these same disorders now affect men, such as anorexia nervosa and bulimia, in the United States.

5. What is the **best** change, if any, to make in the sentence in line 24 (*The American . . . loss nowadays.*)?

   a. Change *public* to **Public**.
   b. Change *preoccupies* to **preoccupied**.
   c. Change *seems* to **seemed**.
   d. Make no change.

6. What is the **best** change, if any, to make in the sentence in lines 10–11 (*They are . . . and weight.*)?

   a. Insert a comma after **and**.
   b. Change *anxious* to **anscious**.
   c. Delete the comma after **food**.
   d. Make no change.

7. Pete wants to add the following sentence to the fourth paragraph: *All-male support groups do exist.* This sentence would **best** fit

   a. after the sentence in lines 21–22 (*Men may . . . that environment.*).
   b. after the sentence in lines 19–20 (*They may . . . or anorexia.*).
   c. after the sentence in lines 18–19 (*In fact . . . eating disorders.*).
   d. after the sentence in line 18 (*Unfortunately, many . . . their problems.*).

8. What is the **best** change, if any, to make in the sentence in lines 8–9 (*Symptoms of . . . of appetite.*)?

   a. Change *lose* to **loss**.
   b. Insert a comma after **combined**.
   c. Change *include* to **includes**.
   d. Make no change.

9. What is the **best** change, if any, to make in the sentence in lines 22–23 (*If a . . . recover successfully.*)?

   a. Change *effective* to **efective**.
   b. Insert a comma after **program**.
   c. Change *he* to **him**.
   d. Make no change.

10. What would be the **best** way to rewrite the sentence in lines 16–17 (*Men suffering . . . stress dieting.*) to make it more specific?

    a. Men suffering from bulimia and anorexia nervosa are often involved in sports, which stress dieting.
    b. Men suffering from bulimia and anorexia nervosa are often engaged in sports where dieting is important.
    c. Men suffering from bulimia and anorexia nervosa are often involved in all kinds of sports that stress dieting.
    d. Men suffering from bulimia and anorexia nervosa are often involved in wrestling, running, and other sports that stress dieting.

LOSING THE PENAN

June's social studies class has been studying Asian countries. Her teacher asks each student to choose a country and to write a report highlighting a particular issue that affects the country. June does some research at the local library and writes her rough draft. She needs your help editing and revising it.

Here is June's rough draft. Read it and then answer questions 1–10.

1 Borneo, located southeast of the Malay Peninsula and southwest of the
2 Philippines, is a mountainous Malaysian island. It is the third largest island in the
3 world. Borneo's climate is hot and wet; portions of the island receive as much as
4 150–200 inches of rainfall each year. Monsoons are not uncommon throughout the
5 fall and winter seasons. With all this rain, Borneo has one of the diversest collections
6 of plants in the world. Rainforests grow densely in certain areas.

7 Over time, Borneo has been home to many different groups. Native tribes still
8 inhabit the island. European explorers and traders began coming during the
9 sixteenth century. Today, the population is a diverse mix of native people, Asians,
10 and europeans. One group in particular, however, is currently threatened by
11 extinction. They are the Penan, who make there home in the state of Sarawak.

12 Native tribes in Borneo rely heavily on the rainforest for their survival. They live
13 on the plants and animals. Nearly all of Sarawak was once covered in forest. More
14 than half of it is licensed for logging. Only about twelve percent of the rainforest has
15 been protected and set aside for national parks and wildlife sanctuaries. As of 1999,
16 seventy percent of the rainforest in Sarawak had been stripped bare. Logging,
17 poaching, and man-made fires in the rainforests in Borneo caused problems for many
18 animals. The population of the red-haired orangutan found only in Borneo dropped
19 from 180,000 to 30,000 in just ten years. It now faces extinction. Sarawak's state
20 bird, the hornbill is also endangered. Many plants did not survive the destructive
21 logging practices. The rivers had been polluted as well.

22 The peaceable Penan nomads are mainly "animists, who believe that nature has
23 a soul and forest spirits must be protected and left undisturbed. They are one of the
24 few hunter-gatherer tribes left in the world today. Just about 260 native Penans
25 were still living in the jungle in 1999, and the logging population largely
26 outnumbered the 260 native Penans. Of the 9,000 Penans in Borneo at that time,
27 most had moved to government settlements, leaving only 63 families left to live in the
28 rainforest. These government settlements were largely described as hot, stifling
29 refugee camps with dirty water.

30 Like the rainforest, the native Penan way of life has been largely infiltrated and
31 destroyed. Western society has slowly crept into Borneo. McDonald's restaurants
32 and cell phones have popped up even on this remote island. Sarawak has become a
33 popular tourist destination. Some remember a quiet, peaceful way of life in the
34 rainforest. One can only hope that them can soon return home.

1. Which of the following is the **best** supporting detail to add after the sentence in lines 14–15 (*Only about . . . wildlife sanctuaries.*)?

    a. Penan tribespeople use poison blowpipes and spears to protect themselves.
    b. The capital of Sarawak is Kuching.
    c. Even these areas, according to environmentalists, are threatened by erosion and river silt.
    d. Sarawak is the size of Mississippi.

2. What is the **best** change, if any, to make in the sentence in lines 22–23 (*The peaceable . . . left undisturbed.*)?

    a. Change *peaceable* to **piecable**.
    b. Insert quotation marks after **animists,**.
    c. Change *has* to **have**.
    d. Make no change.

3. What is the **best** change, if any, to make in the sentence in lines 5–6 (*With all . . . the world.*)?

    a. Change *diversest* to **most diverse**.
    b. Change *world* to **World**.
    c. Delete the comma after **rain**.
    d. Make no change.

4. The topic sentence of the second paragraph is in

    a. line 7 (*Over time . . . different groups.*).
    b. lines 8–9 (*European explorers . . . sixteenth century.*).
    c. lines 9–10 (*Today, the . . . and europeans.*).
    d. line 11 (*They are . . . of Sarawak.*).

5. What is the **best** change, if any, to make in the sentence in line 34 (*One can . . . return home.*)?

    a. Change the *period* to a **question mark**.
    b. Insert a comma after **hope**.
    c. Change *them* to **they**.
    d. Make no change.

6. What is the **best** change, if any, to make in the sentence in lines 9–10 (*Today, the . . . and europeans.*)?

   a. Delete a comma after **Asians**.
   b. Change *europeans* to **Europeans**.
   c. Insert a comma after **mix**.
   d. Make no change.

7. The sentence in lines 18–19 (*The population . . . ten years.*) is poorly written. Which one of these is the **best** way to rewrite it?

   a. From 180,000 to 30,000, in just ten years, the population of the red-haired orangutan found only in Borneo dropped.
   b. Borneo dropped its ten-year population of the red-haired orangutan from 180,000 to 30,000.
   c. Found only in Borneo, the ten red-haired orangutan population dropped from 180,000 to 30,000 in just ten years.
   d. The population of the red-haired orangutan, found only in Borneo, dropped from 180,000 to 30,000 in just ten years.

8. What is the **best** change, if any, to make in the sentence in lines 19–20 (*Sarawak's state . . . also endangered.*)?

   a. Change *Sarawak's* to **Sarawaks'**.
   b. Insert a comma after **hornbill**.
   c. Change *endangered* to **indangered**.
   d. Make no change.

9. What is the **best** change, if any, to make in the sentence in line 11 (*They are . . . of Sarawak.*)?

   a. Change *there* to **their**.
   b. Change *state* to **State**.
   c. Delete the comma after **Penan**.
   d. Make no change.

10. What is the **best** way to rewrite the sentence in lines 24–26 (*Just about . . . native Penans.*) to improve the paragraph?
    a. Just about 260 native Penans were still living in the jungle in 1999, and the logging population, of about 260, outnumbered them.
    b. In 1999, about 260 native Penans were still living in the jungle, and the logging population largely outnumbered the Penans.
    c. The logging population largely outnumbered the approximately 260 native Penans still living in the jungle in 1999.
    d. About 260 native Penans outnumbered the logging population in 1999, largely still living in the jungle.

BLOGGING   36

Stanley's computer class has been studying recent advances in technology. His teacher asks the class to write reports discussing how a current trend is affecting teenagers. Stanley chooses his topic and writes his rough draft. He needs your help editing and revising it.

Here is Stanley's rough draft. Read it and then answer questions 1–10.

1   If your like me, you probably have a blog. If you're not familiar with the term,
2   then let me explain it to you. "Blog" is an abbreviation for "weblog," an expression
3   coined by Jorn Barger, the owner of the long-established Robot Wisdom weblog. A
4   blog is basically an online diary. In the past ten years or so, blogging has become one
5   of the more trendy ways to comunicate over the Internet. Teenagers aged thirteen to
6   nineteen make up more than half of the bloggers in the United States. It's a fun
7   activity and fairly harmless, as long as you take the proper precautions.

8   Keeping a blog allows you to express yourself in a new way. You can be as honest
9   and personal as you like, depending on what you want to include in your blog. Many
10 teenagers use blogs as a way to talk to each other about things in their lives. Blogs
11 are a great way to connect with others. In fact, some teachers are now using blogs
12 as a way to get their students to react to one anothers' work. Teenagers use blogging
13 today like teenagers in the 1980s used the mall—as a place to hang out!

14 *The Mercury News* in San Jose California, did an extensive article on blogging.
15 Reporter K. Oanh Ha told of a fifteen-year-old freshman girl who learned everything
16 she could about a classmate from his blog. She never spoke with him face to face. In
17 fact, she was horrified by the notion. She said "I read his [blog] every day and
18 learned a lot about him." She was able to determine that he was "too weird" after a
19 few months and the two never even spoke. Now I call that a cyber-crush?

20 Blogs aren't difficult to figure out, either. It is inexpensive to get started, and
21 there is special software that makes blogging easy. All you really needs is an Internet
22 connection, the software, and the dedication to keep your blog going over time.

23 Nevertheless, you should use caution when posting your information in a blog.
24 Don't tell weirdos where you're at or what you're into. I'm sure you've heard of cyber-
25 stalking and predation. Its important that you don't expose yourself to dangerous
26 characters looking to take advantage of you.

27 Happy blogging!

1. What is the **best** change, if any, to make in the sentence in lines 21–22 (*All you . . . over time.*)?

   a. Delete the comma after **connection**.
   b. Change *needs* to **need**.
   c. Change *your* to **you're**.
   d. Make no change.

2. What is the **best** change, if any, to make in the sentence in line 14 (*The Mercury . . . on blogging.*)?

   a. Insert a comma after **Jose**.
   b. Delete the comma after **California**.
   c. Change *extensive* to **extenncive**.
   d. Make no change.

3. What is the **best** change, if any, to make in the sentence in lines 4–5 (*In the . . . the Internet.*)?

   a. Change *trendy* to **trendie**.
   b. Insert a comma after **Internet**.
   c. Change *comunicate* to **communicate**.
   d. Make no change.

4. What is the **best** change, if any, to make in the sentence in line 19 (*Now I . . . a cyber-crush?*)?

   a. Change *I* to **me**.
   b. Change the *question mark* to an **exclamation point**.
   c. Change *call* to **calling**.
   d. Make no change.

5. Instead of the sentence in line 24 (*Don't tell . . . you're into.*), which of these uses the **best** tone for this audience?

   a. Don't reveal too many details about your location or other personal matters to strangers.
   b. If you want to broadcast your info all over the Internet, feel free, but don't say I didn't warn you!
   c. Strangers may want you to tell them stuff about you, but watch out.
   d. If you tell people where you are and what you like to do, they're strangers.

6. What is the **best** change, if any, to make in the sentence in line 20 (*Blogs aren't . . . out, either.*)?

    a. Change *either* to **eether**.
    b. Change *aren't* to **wasn't**.
    c. Change *to* to **too**.
    d. Make no change.

7. What is the **best** change, if any, to make in the sentence in line 1 (*If your . . . a blog.*)?

    a. Change *a* to **an**.
    b. Delete the comma after **me**.
    c. Change *your* to **you're**.
    d. Make no change.

8. What is the **best** change, if any, to make in the sentence in lines 17–18 (*She said . . . about him."*)?

    a. Insert a comma after **said**.
    b. Change *him* to **he**.
    c. Delete the quotation marks before **I**.
    d. Make no change.

9. What would be the **best** way to rewrite the sentence in lines 9–10 (*Many teenagers . . . their lives.*) to make it more specific?

    a. Blogs are used by many teenagers to talk to each other about all kinds of stuff.
    b. Many teenagers talk to each other about things in their lives using blogs.
    c. Many teenagers use blogs as a way to talk to communicate with each other on common topics.
    d. Many teenagers use blogs as a way to discuss problems that they're having at home, at school, or in relationships with friends.

10. What is the **best** change, if any, to make in the sentence in lines 11–12 (*In fact . . . anothers' work.*)?

    a. Change *way* to **weigh**.
    b. Change *anothers'* to **another's**.
    c. Change *their* to **there**.
    d. Make no change.

A Coral Feat

The principal of a Florida middle school has asked each student in the seventh grade to write a brief report about a place he or she visited on a field trip in the past school year. The principal is trying to determine where she will take the next class of seventh graders. Juniper chooses to write about the Coral Castle in Homestead. She has written her rough draft and needs your help editing and revising it.

Here is Juniper's rough draft. Read it and then answer questions 1–10.

1 Edward Leedskalnin was born in Riga, Latvia, on August 10 1887. At the age of
2 26, he was engaged to a sixteen-year-old named Agnes Scuffs, whom he called his
3 "Sweet Sixteen." She has been described as Leedskalnin's one true love. Just a day
4 before the wedding was to be held, Scuffs cancelled the ceremony breaking
5 Leedskalnin's heart. In memory of his lost love, this private man created one of the
6 world's most remarkable accomplishments: the Coral Castle.

7 How did the Egyptians move the gigantic stones to create the pyramids? That is
8 a mistory. A similar mystery surrounds the building of Coral Castle in Homestead
9 Florida. It is believed that Leedskalnin single-handedly carved and sculpted over
10 1,100 tons of coral rock. At just five feet tall and weighing merely 100 pounds, this
11 small man somehow cut and moved these immense coral blocks using only hand
12 tools. Prior knowledge from working in lumber camps and in stone masonry helped
13 him to know how to move them.

14 Or did it? Some people believe that he somehow learned the power harnessed by
15 the Egyptians many years ago. They think that he levitated the coral blocks.
16 Leedskalnin himself was quoted as saying, "I have discovered the secrets of the
17 pyramids, and have found out how the Egyptians, . . . with only primitive tools, raised
18 and set in place blocks of stone weighing many tons".

19 Leedskalnin worked at night on his ten-acre plot in southern Florida. Just how
20 he managed to move these coral blocks, some of which weighed as much as 30 tons
21 each, has not yet been discovered. It is said that if he felt himself being watched at
22 his work, he would quit what he was doing.

23 Leedskalnin did not just build a castle structure with walls constructed of 15-ton
24 blocks. He erected a 22-ton obelisk, a three-ton rocking chair, numerous giant
25 puzzles, and sculptures featuring planets and the moon. A 30-ton telescope towers
26 25 feet above the complex. It is perfectly aligned to the north star. A working sundial
27 accurately tells time within two minutes. A 5,000-pound heart-shaped coral rock
28 table is believed to be the largest valentine in the world. Perhaps his most
29 miraculous creation was a nine-ton gate that provides entrance to the castle. The
30 gate is 80 inches wide. It is 92 inches tall. It is 21 inches thick. It is so perfectly
31 balanced on its center of gravity that a person can open it by pushing with just one
32 finger. Incredible!

(continued on next page)

(continued from previous page)

33   It is interesting to note that the area where Coral Castle can be found is in
34 considered part of the Bermuda Triangle. Leedskalnin has been described as highly
35 intuitive and looked for signs of anomaly in nature. His notebooks were filled with
36 drawings and plans for magnetism and electrical experiments. Although he had just
37 a fourth-grade education, he is believed to perhaps have discovered a way to reduce
38 the earth's gravitational pull. Is this possible? Until the mystery surrounding Coral
39 Castle's construction is solved, we will never know.

40   In December 1951, Leedskalnin became ill. He put a sign on his door that said,
41 "going to the Hospital," and took the bus to Jackson Memorial Hospital in Miami. He
42 died three days later in his sleep at the age of 64. It took Ed Leedskalnin 28 years
43 to build this testament of his love for Agnes Scuffs. His spectacular accomplishment
44 will continue to amaze visitors for years to come.

1. What is the **best** change, if any, to make in the sentence in lines 16–18 (*Leedskalnin himself . . . many tons".*)?

    a. Change *primitive* to **primative**.
    b. Delete the comma after **tools**.
    c. Change *tons".* to **tons."**.
    d. Make no change.

2. Which of the following is the **best** way to combine the three sentences in lines 29–30 (*The gate . . . inches thick.*)?

    a. The gate is 80 inches wide, 92 inches tall, and 21 inches thick.
    b. The gate is 80, 90, and 21 inches wide, tall, and thick.
    c. The gate, which is 80 inches wide, is 92 inches tall and 21 inches thick.
    d. At 80 inches wide, 92 inches tall, and 21 inches wide is the gate.

3. What is the **best** change, if any, to make in the sentence in lines 3–5 (*Just a . . . Leedskalnin's heart.*)?

    a. Insert a comma after **ceremony**.
    b. Change *cancelled* to **canceled**.
    c. Change *Scuffs* to **Scuffs's**.
    d. Make no change.

4. What is the **best** change, if any, to make in the sentence in line 26 (*It is . . . north star.*)?

   a. Change *aligned* to **alined**.
   b. Change *north star* to **North Star**.
   c. Change *It* to **He**.
   d. Make no change.

5. The sentence in lines 34–35 (*Leedskalnin has . . . in nature.*) is poorly written. Which one of these is the **best** way to rewrite it?

   a. Leedskalnin looked for signs of anomaly in nature while being a highly intuitive man.
   b. Leedskalnin was both a highly intuitive man and someone who looked for signs of anomaly in nature.
   c. Leedskalnin has been described as a highly intuitive man who looked for signs of anomaly in nature.
   d. Leedskalnin's highly intuitive nature halped him look for signs of anomaly.

6. What is the **best** change, if any, to make in the sentence in lines 7–8 (*That . . . mistory.*)?

   a. Change *is* to **am**.
   b. Change the *period* to a **question mark**.
   c. Change *mistory* to **mystery**.
   d. Make no change.

7. What is the **best** change, if any, to make in the sentence in lines 40–41 (*He put . . . in Miami.*)?

   a. Change *"going* to **"Going**.
   b. Change *took* to **had taken**.
   c. Delete the comma after **said**.
   d. Make no change.

8. What is the **best** way to rewrite the sentence in lines 23–24 (*Leedskalnin did . . . 15-ton blocks.*) to improve the paragraph?

   a. Leedskalnin did not just build a castle structure with constructed walls of 15-ton blocks.
   b. Leedskalnin built a castle structure with walls of 15-ton blocks.
   c. Leedskalnin not just built a castle with walls constructed of 15-ton blocks.
   d. Leedskalnin did not just construct a castle with walls of 15-ton blocks.

9. What is the **best** change, if any, to make in the sentence in line 1 (*Edward Leedskalnin . . . 10 1887.*)?

   a. Change *Riga* to **riga**.
   b. Insert a comma after **10**.
   c. Delete the comma after **Riga**.
   d. Make no change.

10. What is the **best** change, if any, to make in the sentence in lines 33–34 (*It is . . . Bermuda Triangle.*)?

    a. Coral Castle can, interestingly enough, be found in a considered part of the Bermuda Triangle.
    b. Finding the Bermuda Triangle within Coral Castle is an interesting consideration, in part, to note.
    c. Interestingly, the area where Coral Castle can be found is considered part of the Bermuda Triangle.
    d. Noting that the area where Coral Castle can be found is considered part of the Bermuda Triangle is interesting.

Is Stretching Unnecessary?

Shane's seventh-grade health class has been studying fitness. His teacher has asked that each student write a report on a topic related to fitness and exercise. Shane chooses his topic, visits the library, and writes his rough draft. He needs your help editing and revising it.

Here is Shane's rough draft. Read it and then answer questions 1–10.

1 Many runners thinking that they are preventing injury, stretch their muscles
2 before heading out to run. However, new research shows that some runners get hurt
3 more because they stretch. A study conducted by Dr. David A. Lally of the University
4 of Hawaii at manoa backs this idea.

5 Dr. Lally surveyed 1,543 runners participating in the Honolulu Marathon. He
6 found that high-mileage runners and those who worked out for long periods of time
7 were more likely to be injured. While low-mileage, short-duration runners less likely.
8 (An injury in this case is damage done to the body that would prohibit usual training
9 for at least five days). Perhaps these findings are not that surprising. However, what
10 may be more surprising is Dr. Lally's discovery that stretching is also linked with
11 more injuries.

12 Dr. Lally's survey found that 47 percent of the male runners who regularly
13 stretched were hurt during the past year. This percentage was made up entirely of
14 white men. Of those who didn't stretch, only 33 percent suffered an injury. In
15 women, however, Dr. Lally found that those who stretched had the same rate of
16 injury as those women who did not. Of the Asians included in the survey, the amount
17 of stretching affected neither men nor women.

18 When interviewed by *Peak Performance* magazine, Dr. Lally could not explain
19 why stretching and injuries in white males should be so closely related. He said, "but
20 there's certainly no . . . reason why stretching should limit injury risk. After all, most
21 running injuries are caused by overuse, and stretching your muscles before workouts
22 is not going to prevent you overusing them.

23 The time when the stretches are done could factor in. Those runners who
24 stretched after they ran, instead of before, had fewer of injuries when compared to
25 those who didn't stretch at all. Muscles are usually fairly tight when you finish
26 exercising. Stretching at the end of a workout could relax the fibers in the muscles.
27 You will then be better prepared for regular daily activities.

28 Dr. Lallys' survey provides an intriguing view for runners. Of course, every
29 person's body is different and each athlete should make an educated decision
30 regarding his or her best stretching routine. Next time you go out for a run, think
31 about what your body might be trying to tell you.

1. Which transition would **best** fit at the beginning of the sentence in line 26 (*Stretching at . . . the muscles.*)?

    a. For example,
    b. Therefore,
    c. Next,
    d. In other words,

2. What is the **best** change, if any, to make in the sentence in lines 3–4 (*A study . . . this idea.*)?

    a. Change *manoa* to **Manoa**.
    b. Change *conducted* to **conduckted**.
    c. Insert a comma after **Lally**.
    d. Make no change.

3. What is the **best** change, if any, to make in the sentence in line 28 (*Dr. Lallys' . . . for runners.*)?

    a. Change *intriguing* to **intreeging**.
    b. Change *provides* to **provide**.
    c. Change *Lallys'* to **Lally's**.
    d. Make no change.

4. Which of the following is the **best** closing sentence for the third paragraph?

    a. Dr. Lally's survey was filled with inconclusive data.
    b. Men and women of all races were found to have the same rate of injury if they stretched before running the marathon.
    c. Asians refused to stretch, which explains why they were not included in the survey.
    d. Overall, Dr. Lally found the highest connection between stretching and injury in white males.

5. What is the **best** change, if any, to make in the sentence in lines 20–22 (*After all . . . overusing them.*)?

    a. Insert quotation marks after **them.**
    b. Change *overusing* to **overuseing**.
    c. Change *your* to **you're**.
    d. Make no change.

6. Where is there an incomplete sentence?

    a. in line 9 (*Perhaps these . . . that surprising.*)
    b. in lines 28–30 (*Of course . . . stretching routine.*)
    c. in line 7 (*While low-mileage . . . less likely.*)
    d. in lines 25–26 (*Muscles are . . . finish exercising.*)

7. The sentence in lines 9–11 (*However, what . . . more injuries.*) is poorly written. Which one of these is the **best** way to rewrite it?

    a. What may be more surprising is that Dr. Lally discovered that stretching is also linked with more injuries.
    b. What Dr. Lally discovered may be more surprising, however, when it pertains to injuries and stretching.
    c. More surprising is Dr. Lally's discovery that links higher amounts of stretching with a higher frequency of injuries.
    d. Injuries and stretching may be linked by Dr. Lally's more surprising discovery.

8. What is the **best** change, if any, to make in the sentence in lines 1–2 (*Many runners . . . to run.*)?

    a. Insert a comma after **muscles**.
    b. Insert a comma after **runners**.
    c. Insert a comma after **before**.
    d. Make no change.

9. What is the **best** change, if any, to make in the sentence in lines 8–9 [(*An injury . . . five days*).]?

    a. Change *training* to **trayning**.
    b. Change *days).* to **days.).**.
    c. Insert a comma after **damage**.
    d. Make no change.

10. What is the **best** change, if any, to make in the sentence in lines 19–20 (*He said . . . injury risk.*)?

    a. Change *there's* to **theirs**.
    b. Insert a comma after **stretching**.
    c. Change *"but* to **"But**.
    d. Make no change.

THE DWARF GECKO 39

Alaya's seventh-grade science class is studying reptiles and amphibians. Her teacher has asked each student to write a report about one reptile or amphibian. Alaya does her research and writes her rough draft. She needs your help editing and revising it.

Here is Alaya's rough draft. Read it and then answer questions 1–10.

1 In a cave deep in a partially destroyed forest in jaragua national park, the
2 smallest living lizard species lay hidden. It wasn't until 2001 that biologists
3 discovered it. The Jaragua Sphaero, or dwarf gecko, is the world's smallest lizard
4 among 23,000 known species of birds, mammals, and reptiles.

5 The scientific name of the dwarf gecko, *Sphaerodactylus ariasae*, is named after
6 Yvonne Arias. She was head of the Dominican conservation organization, Grupo
7 Jaragua. Blair Hedges of Pennsylvania State University and Richard Thomas of the
8 University of Puerto Rico, found this new species within the national park on Beata
9 Island, which is in the Dominican Republic. The dwarf gecko measures just two
10 centimeters from nose to tail and weighs a mere .00455 ounces. It comfortably fits
11 on a U.S. dime. Dr. Hedges said that finding the gecko was a surprising discovery.
12 He was reminded that us do not know everything about the Earth around us. In an
13 area heavily studied for hundreds of years, it is amazing and wonderful that new
14 species can still be found.

15 The Caribbean Islands feature both the smallest and largest of some other species
16 as well. There are fewer species to compete with, so these unique birds, mammals,
17 and reptiles appear. The world's smallest bird, the Bee Hummingbird is merely five
18 centimeters long. It is found only in Cuba. A frog measured just one centimeter can
19 also be found in Cuba. The West Indies feature the world's smallest snake, the
20 Lesser Antillean Threadsnake. This snake could make it's way through the path left
21 in a pencil if the lead were removed.

22 While the Caribbean is one of the best places on the planet to find unique species,
23 overpopulation and logging practices threaten that natchural environment.
24 Immediately upon being found, the dwarf gecko was declared an endangered species.
25 It makes I wonder how many other species have come and gone without ever having
26 been discovered.

1. What is the **best** change, if any, to make in the sentence in lines 25–26 (*It makes . . . been discovered.*)?

   a. Change *I* to **me**.
   b. Change *having been* to **had**.
   c. Insert a comma after **come**.
   d. Make no change.

2. What is the **best** change, if any, to make in the sentence in lines 1–2 (*In a . . . lay hidden.*)?

   a. Change *lay* to **lied**.
   b. Insert a comma after **partly**.
   c. Change *jaragua national park* to **Jaragua National Park**.
   d. Make no change.

3. What is the **best** change, if any, to make in the sentence in lines 7–9 (*Blair Hedges . . . Dominican Republic.*)?

   a. Change *Dominican Republic* to **dominican republic**.
   b. Delete the comma after **Rico**.
   c. Change the *period* to an **exclamation point**.
   d. Make no change.

4. What is the **best** way to rewrite the sentence in lines 5–6 (*The scientific . . . Yvonne Arias.*) to improve the paragraph?

   a. The scientific name of the dwarf gecko, *Sphaerodactylus ariasae*, comes from Yvonne Arias.
   b. *Sphaerodactylus ariasae*, the scientific name of the dwarf gecko, is just like Yvonne Arias's name.
   c. The dwarf gecko's scientific name, *Sphaerodactylus ariasae*, refers to Yvonne Arias.
   d. *Sphaerodactylus ariasae* is the dwarf gecko's scientific name, which is named after Yvonne Arias.

5. What is the **best** change, if any, to make in the sentence in lines 22–23 (*While the . . . natchural environment.*)?

   a. Change *natchural* to **natural**.
   b. Insert a comma after **overpopulation**.
   c. Change *is* to **are**.
   d. Make no change.

6. What is the **best** change, if any, to make in the sentence in line 12 (*He was . . . around us.*)?

   a. Change *reminded* to **remind**.
   b. Change *that us* to **that we**.
   c. Change *around us* to **around we**.
   d. Make no change.

7. What is the **best** change, if any, to make in the sentence in lines 17–18 (*The world's . . . centimeters long.*)?

   a. Change *merely* to **meerly**.
   b. Insert a comma after **Hummingbird**.
   c. Change the *period* to a **question mark**.
   d. Make no change.

8. The sentence in lines 16–17 (*There are . . . reptiles appear.*) is poorly written. Which one of these is the **best** way to rewrite it?

   a. Species competing less makes more unique birds, mammals, and reptiles appear.
   b. With fewer species to compete with, unique birds, mammals, and reptiles appear.
   c. Fewer species competing means more appearing unique birds, mammals, and reptiles.
   d. There are fewer species with which to compete, so more unique birds, mammals, and reptiles appear.

9. What is the **best** change, if any, to make in the sentence in lines 18–19 (*A frog . . . in Cuba.*)?

   a. Change *measured* to **measuring**.
   b. Insert a comma after **centimeter**.
   c. Change *can also be* to **could also been**.
   d. Make no change.

10. What is the **best** change, if any, to make in the sentence in lines 20–21 (*This snake . . . were removed.*)?

    a. Change *lead* to **ledd**.
    b. Change *it's* to **its**.
    c. Insert a comma after **pencil**.
    d. Make no change.

New Coke

Rick's seventh-grade social studies class has been studying trends in contemporary society. His teacher has asked each student to choose a trend from the past fifty years and write a report about it. Rick visits his local library and writes his rough draft. He needs your help editing and revising it.

Here is Rick's rough draft. Read it and then answer questions 1–10.

1 The Coca-Cola company did an experiment on the North American soft-drink
2 lover beginning on April 23, 1985. Launching "New Coke" with the slogan, "The Best
3 Just Got Better," the company ended the production of the much-loved original Coca-
4 Cola product and replaced it with a new formula. They made a mistake in not asking
5 testing groups whether or not they would be interested in a new Coke product.

6 What made Coke decide to launch New Coke! Product testers found that more
7 people preferred the sweeter taste of Pepsi. The two companies had been competing
8 for customers for many years. Coca-Cola's popularity had been shrinking since World
9 War II. In fact, the only thing keeping Coke afloat was that it was available in more
10 vending machines and fast-food restaurants. Newer products were making the
11 market tougher on cola sales. These other beverages included those manufactured
12 by the Coca-Cola and Pepsi companies.

13 Diet Coke was first released in 1982. It became an instant success with its
14 smoother flavor. In fact, Diet Coke's taste was similarer to Pepsi than to the original
15 formula for Coca-Cola. By 1984, Diet Coke was number three among soft drinks in
16 America. Taste tests were held to determine if Coke or Pepsi was the preferred cola
17 beverage among Americans. People liked Pepsi better.

18 New Coke was developed and tested and tasted smoother and sweeter than
19 original Coke and was more like Pepsi. Blind taste tests showed that people who
20 tasted the experimental beverage claimed to like it better than original Coke or
21 Pepsi. It appeared that the Coca-Cola company had a winner. The company decided
22 to discontinue production of original Coke when they released New Coke.

23 So what happened? In blind taste tests, people had loved the new formula. What
24 the company didn't realize was that Coca-Cola's advertising campaign had
25 successfully convinced the American public that original Coke was a central part of
26 being American. When the company released New Coke people who hadn't even
27 tasted it (and those who had) said they hated it. They disliked the taste. They were
28 also unhappy that them could no longer buy the original Coke product. By not asking
29 test subjects how they would feel if a new cola replaced the old one, the Coca-Cola
30 company had made a huge mistake.

31 On July 11, 1985, two Coca-Cola executives made an announcement: We have
32 heard you." People's attachment to the original Coke product was a factor they had
33 not accounted for during all their endless tests and marketing analyses. The

(continued on next page)

(continued from previous page)

34 company re-released the original formula as Coca-Cola Classic, or Classic Coke. The
35 news was so big that Peter Jennings interrupted "General Hospital" to make the
36 announcement on national television. The demand for the product grows and Coke
37 soon beat out Pepsi in the market.

38   Some people believe that the Coca-Cola company knew all along that this "New
39 Coke" idea would result in better sales in the long run. Some think this is a foolish
40 idea, and believe that the company truly thought New Coke would be a success.

1. What is the **best** change, if any, to make in the sentence in lines 26–27 (*When the . . . hated it.*)?

    a. Change *had* to **have**.
    b. Insert a comma after **Coke**.
    c. Change *released* to **releesed**.
    d. Make no change.

2. What is the **best** change, if any, to make in the sentence in lines 14–15 (*In fact . . . for Coca-Cola.*)?

    a. Change *than* to **then**.
    b. Insert a comma after **Pepsi**.
    c. Change *similarer* to **more similar**.
    d. Make no change.

3. The sentence in lines 18–19 (*New Coke . . . like Pepsi.*) is poorly written. Which one of these is the **best** way to rewrite it?

    a. New Coke was developed and tested, and was found to taste smoother and sweeter than the original Coke. In fact, it was more like Pepsi.
    b. New Coke developed and tested a new smoother, sweeter taste that was more like Pepsi and less than the original Coke.
    c. New Coke was developed and tested and was more like Pepsi. It had a smoother, sweeter taste than original Coke.
    d. New Coke was more like Pepsi with its smoother sweeter taste. It was developed and tested more than the original Coke.

4. What is the **best** change, if any, to make in the sentence in lines 27–28 (*They were . . . Coke product.*)?

   a. Change *product* to **Product**.
   b. Change *them* to **they**.
   c. Change *could* to **can**.
   d. Make no change.

5. Which transition would best fit at the beginning of the sentence in lines 4–5 (*They made . . . Coke product.*)?

   a. For example,
   b. In fact,
   c. Moreover,
   d. However,

6. What is the **best** change, if any, to make in the sentence in lines 36–37 (*The demand . . . the market.*)?

   a. Change *grows* to **grew**.
   b. Change *market* to **marcket**.
   c. Insert a comma after **Coke**.
   d. Make no change.

7. What is the **best** change, if any, to make in the sentence in line 6 (*What made . . . New Coke!*)?

   a. Change *launch* to **lawnch**.
   b. Change *made* to **makes**.
   c. Change the *exclamation point* to a **question mark**.
   d. Make no change.

8. Which of the following is the **best** way to combine the two sentences in lines 10–12 (*Newer products . . . Pepsi companies.*)?

   a. Newer products were making the market tougher on cola sales, whose other beverages included those manufactured by the Coca-Cola and Pepsi companies.
   b. The Coca-Cola and Pepsi companies were manufacturing other beverages that made the newer products on the market tougher on cola sales.
   c. The market was tougher on the Coca-Cola and Pepsi companies, who were making newer products that were tougher on cola sales.
   d. Plus, newer products, including those manufactured by the Coca-Cola and Pepsi companies, were making the market tougher on cola sales.

9. What is the **best** change, if any, to make in the sentence in lines 31–32 (*On July . . . heard you."*)?

   a. Change *heard* to **hear**.
   b. Insert quotation marks before **We**.
   c. Change *executives* to **Executives**.
   d. Make no change.

10. The sentence in lines 32–33 (*People's attachment . . . marketing analyses.*) is poorly written. Which one of these is the **best** way to rewrite it?

    a. People's attachment to the endless tests and marketing analyses could not account for the original Coke product.
    b. People were attached to the original Coke product, but only after endless tests and marketing analyses.
    c. Endless tests and marketing analyses did not account for or predict people's attachment to the original Coke product.
    d. The original Coke product was so much of a factor during all their endless tests and marketing analyses that they could not remember the people's attachment.

THE JUGGLING INMATES 41

Reginald's seventh-grade social studies class has been studying different means of communicating. His teacher has asked each student to write a report about a form of communication. Reginald does some research and writes his rough draft. He needs your help editing and revising it.

Here is Reginald's rough draft. Read it and then answer questions 1–10.

1 Jim Carlson, the head of the arts program in San Quentin California, made a
2 unique decision; he wanted to take juggling to prisons. He felt that juggling forced
3 people to work together, while keeping a rhythm going. When Sara Felder first
4 moved to San Quentin, she worked with Carlson. Felder enrolled in Carlson's
5 juggling program.

6 Carlson's program was soon underway. The men Felder had volunteered to work
7 with in the maximum-security prison in San Quentin were often pensive. The facility
8 was mostly populated with inmates who were serving life sentences. While Felder
9 admits to being frightened by the environment at first, she said she never felt unsafe
10 with the inmates. She treated them like human beings and, naturally, liked some
11 more than others.

12 By working together and being patient, the inmates seemed to take to juggling
13 right away. A man serving a life sentence learns pretty quickly that all he has left is
14 time. Few of these inmates appeared to grow impatient when they couldn't
15 immediately learn a trick. The men learned grace, flexibility, and beauty.
16 Meanwhile, Felder realizes that learning juggling was a positive experience for these
17 men who, for much of their lives, had known failure and defeat. Succeeding at
18 juggling and trying something new was an exceedingly rewarding experience—for
19 both the men and they're teacher. The inmates worked very hard to get it right. As
20 Felder remembers it, they created "beauty in a pretty ugly place."

21 The security at the facility in San Quentin was changed to minimum, which
22 altered its atmosphere. While Felder often found working with inmates in for life
23 sentences to be very rewarding, she found that most inmates serving shorter periods
24 of time were not interested in learning about juggling or working together. Some
25 would try it to pass the time or to teach it to their children when they were released.
26 It wasn't about being creative for these inmates; it was more of a hobby.

27 Felder's next volunteer assignment was in vacaville in a maximum-security
28 prison for the mentally and physically ill. Felder described this prison as a "black
29 hole . . . just desperate energy and it was all contained." She said that since there
30 was so much "crazy" activity, juggling just seemed to fit in. Mentally ill patients who
31 didn't seem to understand a word that was being said to them would calmly take
32 objects and start juggling them. Slowly, some of the inmates would grow proud of
33 their accomplishments. Juggling was a healthy means of communicating. A way to
34 keep their brains active.

(continued on next page)

(continued from previous page)

> 35   As of 1996, Sara Felder was working at a halfway house in San Francisco. The
> 36 facility was for men and women who had recently been released from prison or who
> 37 were on parole, some of whom were dealing with addictions. She was teaching
> 38 theater and clowning, which includes juggling. The ex-convicts in her troupe
> 39 performed for little kids. These activities filled Felder with a growing sense of pride.
>
> 40   While Sara Felder wasn't sure she still had it in her to return to teaching in
> 41 prison, the benefits of learning from a diverse group of people had not completely
> 42 evaporated. She said, "I always learn a lot and I think I have something to give to
> 43 them, but it might be someone else's turn to take it over. . . . I think I paid a price.
> 44 Emotionally, physically, I think it was hard. . . . I think for a lot of us, juggling has
> 45 saved our lives".

1. What is the **best** change, if any, to make in the sentence in lines 16–17 (*Meanwhile, Felder . . . and defeat.*)?

    a. Change *their* to **they're**.
    b. Change *realizes* to **realized**.
    c. Change *failure* to **failyre**.
    d. Make no change.

2. Where is there an incomplete sentence?

    a. in lines 33–34 (*A way . . . brains active.*)
    b. in lines 14–15 (*Few of . . . a trick.*)
    c. in line 43 (*I think . . . a price.*)
    d. in lines 7–8 (*The facility . . . life sentences.*)

3. What is the **best** change, if any, to make in the sentence in lines 1–2 (*Jim Carlson . . . to prisons.*)?

    a. Change the *semi-colon* to a **question mark**.
    b. Insert a comma after **Quentin**.
    c. Remove the comma after **California**.
    d. Make no change.

4. What is the **best** change, if any, to make in the sentence in lines 40–42 (*While Sara . . . completely evaporated.*)?

   a. Change *diverse* to **diverss**.
   b. Insert a comma after **people**.
   c. Change *to return* to **returning**.
   d. Make no change.

5. The sentence in lines 22–24 (*While Felder . . . working together.*) is poorly written. Which one of these is the **best** way to rewrite it?

   a. While working with inmates serving life sentences was very rewarding, Felder found that fewer of those serving shorter terms were interested in learning about juggling or working together.
   b. Working with inmates serving life sentences was much like those serving shorter sentences because they were both interested in juggling and working together.
   c. Felder thought that while inmates serving life sentences were very rewarding, those serving for shorter periods of time were learning juggling and working together.
   d. Inmates serving for shorter periods of time were interested in learning juggling and working together, while those inmates serving life sentences were being rewarded.

6. What is the **best** change, if any, to make in the sentence in lines 27–28 (*Felder's next . . . physically ill.*)?

   a. Change *volunteer* to **vollunteer**.
   b. Insert a comma after **prison**.
   c. Change *vacaville* to **Vacaville**.
   d. Make no change.

7. Which of the following is the **best** way to combine the two sentences in lines 6–8 (*The men . . . life sentences.*)?

   a. Felder volunteered to work with men in the maximum-security prison in San Quentin who were serving life sentences and pensive.
   b. In the maximum-security prison in San Quentin, the men who were serving life sentences in the prison, who Felder volunteered to work with, were pensive.
   c. The pensive men in the maximum-security prison in San Quentin, most of whom were serving life sentences, were the ones that Felder volunteered to work with.
   d. The men that Felder volunteered to work with in the maximum-security prison in San Quentin, most of whom were serving life sentences, were often pensive.

8. What is the **best** change, if any, to make in the sentence in lines 17–19 (*Succeeding at . . . they're teacher.*)?

   a. Change *they're* to **their**.
   b. Change *Succeeding* to **Succeeded**.
   c. Remove the comma after **lives**.
   d. Make no change.

9. What is the **best** change, if any, to make in the sentence in lines 44–45 (*I think . . . our lives".*)?

   a. Change *us* to **we**.
   b. Change *think* to **thinks**.
   c. Change *lives".* to **lives."**.
   d. Make no change.

10. Which of the following is the **best** supporting detail to add after the sentence in line 26 (*It wasn't . . . a hobby.*)?

    a. Felder really enjoyed working with these inmates much more.
    b. Felder found that teaching these inmates became a less than meaningful experience for her and for them.
    c. Teaching these inmates was a lot like teaching the men who were in for life sentences.
    d. The prison, don't forget, was in San Quentin, California.

Jean-Jacques Rousseau

Heloise's seventh-grade French class has been studying eighteenth-century French philosophers. Her teacher has asked the students in the class to write reports on one of the philosophers they have been discussing. Heloise visits the library, composes an outline, and writes her report. She needs your help editing and revising it.

Here is Heloise's rough draft. Read it and then answer questions 1–10.

1   Jean-Jacques Rousseau, philosopher and author, has been called undisciplined.
2 He has also been called a brilliant, original thinker. He is beyond a doubt one of the
3 most controversial, forward-thinking philosophers of the eighteenth century.

4   Rousseau was born in Geneva on June 28, 1712. His mother died while giving
5 birth to him, and his violent, depressed father deserted him when he was just sixteen
6 years old. Rousseau became an apprentice to a notary and then to a coppersmith. In
7 1728, however, he ran away to escape the disciplined lifestyle. After wandering for
8 several days, priests in Savoy turned him, who sent him to a school, over to Madame
9 de Warens. He worked in several households before settling with Madame de Warens
10 in Chambery in 1730. He studied nature, mathematics, latin, and music. He read
11 English, German, and French philosophy and chemistry. He became interested in
12 opera and theater.

13   Rousseau traveled to Paris where he wrote a failed opera called *Les Muses*
14 *Galantes*. He also copied music for a living and was a secretery to Madame Dupin.
15 He fathered several illegitimate children, but refused to support them. While in his
16 forties, he began working as an author.

17   During the French revolution, Rousseau's writings were highly controversial. He
18 first attracted attention with the prize-winning essay, *Discourse on the Sciences and*
19 *the Arts* published in 1750. He thought modern civilization did more harm than good.
20 He described it as artificial and corrupt. He thought that people would benefit more
21 by returning back to nature. He also claimed that pursuing the arts and sciences
22 degraded people's morals. He felt that error and prejudice smothered reason and
23 nature.

24   In 1762, he published *Émile, on education*. He proposed a method of education
25 that would be better for students. The French parliament ordered that *Émile* should
26 be burned and Rousseau should be arrested. He fled to Prussia and then to the Isle
27 St. Pierre. When the government of the Isle St. Pierre ordered him out of the
28 territory. He moved in with another philosopher and author, David Hume, in
29 England. Rousseau had grown paranoid and suspicious. He left England to return
30 to France.

31   Rousseau's 1755 *Discourse on the Origin and Foundation of Inequality Among*
32 *Mankind* applied his theories to politics. He felt that a lot of politicians and
33 intellectuals had a messed up way of looking at things, so then a lot of other people

(continued on next page)

(continued from previous page)

```
34  suffered. In 1762, he proposed The Social Contract as the solution to problems
35  discussed in his Discourse. He described his idea that all men are born free and
36  equal. He said that all citizens agree to be protected by a governing body. However,
37  they do not give up their basic rights to it.
38      Rousseau wrote Confessions, an autobiography of his unstable life, which he
39  wrote throughout his life. It was published in 1783, five years after Rousseau died
40  in Ermenonville.
```

1. What is the **best** way to rewrite the sentence in lines 38–39 (*Rousseau wrote . . . his life.*) to improve the paragraph?

   a. Rousseau wrote *Confessions* throughout his life, which was an autobiography of his unstable life.
   b. *Confessions*, an autobiography of his unstable life, was written throughout Rousseau's life.
   c. Rousseau's *Confessions*, throughout his life, was an autobiography of his unstable life.
   d. Throughout the years of his unstable life, Rousseau wrote an autobiography entitled *Confessions*.

2. What is the **best** change, if any, to make in the sentence in line 17 (*During the . . . highly controversial.*)?

   a. Change *revolution* to **Revolution**.
   b. Change *controversial* to **contravershal**.
   c. Remove the comma after *revolution*.
   d. Make no change.

3. Heloise wants to add the following sentence to the fifth paragraph: *He even fought with his close friends because they would not make his enemies their enemies.* The sentence would **best** fit

   a. after the sentence in lines 25–26 (*The French . . . be arrested.*).
   b. after the sentence in lines 27–28 (*When the . . . the territory.*).
   c. after the sentence in line 29 (*Rousseau had . . . and suspicious.*).
   d. after the sentence in lines 29–30 (*He left . . . to France.*).

4. What is the **best** change, if any, to make in the sentence in line 14 (*He also . . . Madame Dupin.*)?

   a. Change *Madame* to **madame**.
   b. Change *secretery* to **secretary**.
   c. Insert a comma after **also**.
   d. Make no change.

5. What would be the **best** way to rewrite the sentence in lines 24–25 (*He proposed . . . for students.*) to make it more specific?

   a. He proposed a method of education that would benefit the students.
   b. He proposed a method of education to explore and support students' strengths, rather than to hold them back.
   c. He proposed a method of education that would enhance the students' educational experience.
   d. He proposed a method of education that would make things more exciting and interesting for the students.

6. What is the **best** change, if any, to make in the sentence in lines 17–19 (*He first . . . in 1750.*)?

   a. Change *Discourse on the Sciences and the Arts* to discourse on the sciences and the arts.
   b. Remove the comma after **essay**.
   c. Insert a comma after **Arts**.
   d. Make no change.

7. Where is there an incomplete sentence?

   a. in lines 9–10 (*He worked . . . in 1730.*)
   b. in lines 39–40 (*It was . . . in Ermenonville.*)
   c. in lines 27–28 (*When the . . . the territory.*)
   d. in lines 14–15 (*He fathered . . . support them.*)

8. What is the **best** change, if any, to make in the sentence in line 10 (*He studied . . . and music.*)?

   a. Change *latin* to **Latin**.
   b. Change the *period* to a **question mark**.
   c. Change *mathematics* to **mathmatics**.
   d. Make no change.

9. The sentence in lines 7–9 (*After wandering . . . de Warens.*) is poorly written. Which one of these is the **best** way to rewrite it?

   a. After wandering for several days, Madame de Warens and the priests in Savoy turned him over to a school.
   b. After wandering for several days, priests in Savoy turned him over to Madame de Warens, who sent him to a school.
   c. Priests in Savoy, who after several days found him wandering, turned him over to Madame de Warens, who then sent him to a school.
   d. Madame de Warens sent him to a school, while priests in Savoy wandered for several days.

10. Instead of the sentence in lines 32–34 (*He felt . . . people suffered.*), which of these uses the **best** tone for this audience?

    a. He felt that politicians and intellectuals didn't have a clue when it came to what was good for other people.
    b. He felt that many politicians and intellectuals were bad.
    c. He felt that people suffered because politicians and intellectuals were a mess.
    d. He felt that flawed political and intellectual thinking caused most of the human injustice in the world.

No More Censorship! 43

Manuel has been asked by his seventh-grade history teacher to write a report about an event or practice in the United States that conflicts with the following statement by Dwight D. Eisenhower: "[We should] not try to conceal the thinking of our own people. They are part of America. And even if they think ideas that are contrary to ours, their right to say them, their right to record them, and their right to have them at places where they're accessible to others is unquestioned, or it's not America." Manuel maps out a web of ideas and writes his rough draft. He needs your help editing and revising it.

Here is Manuel's rough draft. Read it and then answer questions 1–10.

1   Imagine that your at your local library perusing the fiction shelves. Your eye
2   wanders over the brightly-colored spines. Suddenly, you start to notice that some of
3   the books are disappearing. The time-honored favorites that you've enjoyed reading
4   are beginning to fade away. Could this really happen.

5   The short answer is yes. Censorship in the United States has long been a problem.
6   When it affects you and your freedoms, it's your responsibility to speak up. Librarians
7   do their fair share of fighting against special interest groups who target so-called
8   indecent literature. To be truly effective, we must all take part in the battle for the
9   freedom to read what we chose. Our First Amendment rights of free speech and free
10 press are violated every time a book is challenged or banned. Protect your rights!

11 Living in America grants us another freedom, the freedom of information. We are
12 at liberty to access information from almost anywhere. Some of the books with
13 controversial or disturbing subjects have been banned or challenged for their
14 presentation of these subjects. People deserve to be given the choice to disregard or
15 take note of any information that they encounter.

16 Today, kids seem to spend so much time in front of the television or on the
17 computer. Reading is a healthy, stimulating activity that should be fostered, and not
18 smothered. Strengthening the family bond through reading, books bring adults and
19 children together as well. Some topics are just not easy to discuss with others. Often,
20 after reading about an awkward subject in a book, a child will feel more comfortable
21 discussing it with a friend or family member. Censors seek to protect children by
22 warding off what they perceive as harmful to others, thereby taking away their right
23 to decide for themselves.

24 Just as each one of us has the right to express him- or herself, censors share the
25 same freedom. They're not totally wrong, but they do it wrong. We have an
26 obligation to protect our rights and challenge those who challenge us. The survival
27 of the Democratic way of life hangs in the balance.

28 The number of books challenged has increased over the past few years. Nancy
29 Kranich, president of the American Library Association from 2000–2001, had this to
30 say about the rise in censorship: "each time a book is challenged, restricted, removed,

(continued on next page)

(continued from previous page)

31 or banned, creators are less likely to express themselves.... Teachers and librarians
32 ... risk their jobs and reputation when they dare to confront controversies over the
33 public's right to read." We absolutely cannot take this freedom for granted. We live
34 in a democratic society so that we can enjoy this basic right. Imagine not being able
35 to read what you wanted to! What if you couldn't read award-winning novels like the
36 books in the *Harry Potter* series, *The Adventures of Huckleberry Finn*, *A Wrinkle in*
37 *Time*, or any of your other favorites? We cannot allow others to deny us the freedoms
38 granted in the Bill of Rights.

39   There is a reason why America stands apart from other nations and treasures its
40 freedom of expression. We cannot allow censorship of books or any other media to
41 continue. We can expect a very different America from the one we know today.
42 Technology moves us rapidly ahead, but we must remain aware of the history that
43 gave us the ability to think and act as we do. We must be free to ask questions, study,
44 and evaluate the world around us without being restricted.

1. Instead of the sentence in line 25 (*They're not ... it wrong.*), which of these uses the **best** tone for the audience?

   a. I hate them and their ideas!
   b. Censorship may be wrong, but only because it limits other people's freedoms.
   c. It's like they don't always do it right, but then they turn around and mess around with other people's lives.
   d. Their views are not necessarily wrong, but they can often have a negative impact on others' rights and freedoms.

2. What is the **best** change, if any, to make in the sentence in line 1 (*Imagine that ... fiction shelves.*)?

   a. Change *that your* to **that you're**.
   b. Change *shelves* to **shelfs**.
   c. Change *library* to **Library**.
   d. Make no change.

3. Which transition would **best** fit at the beginning of the sentence in line 41 (*We can ... know today.*)?

   a. For example,
   b. However,
   c. Otherwise,
   d. Nevertheless,

4. What is the **best** change, if any, to make in the sentence in lines 26–27 (*The survival . . . the balance.*)?

   a. Change *Democratic* to **democratic**.
   b. Change *hangs* to **hanged**.
   c. Insert a comma after **survival**.
   d. Make no change.

5. What is the **best** change, if any, to make in the sentence in lines 12–14 (*Some of . . . these subjects.*)?

   a. Some of the books with controversial or disturbing subjects presented banned or challenged material.
   b. Some of the banned or challenged books were chosen for their presentation of controversial or disturbing subjects.
   c. The banned and challenged books presented controversial, disturbing subjects that had been banned or challenged.
   d. Pretty much all of the challenged books were disturbing and controversial to anyone who read them.

6. What is the **best** change, if any, to make in the sentence in line 4 (*But could . . . really happen.*)?

   a. Change *could* to **had been**.
   b. Change the *period* to a **question mark**.
   c. Insert a comma after **But**.
   d. Make no change.

7. Which of the following is the **best** way to combine the two sentences in lines 34–37 (*Imagine not . . . other favorites?*)?

   a. What if you couldn't read *The Adventures of Huckleberry Finn*, *A Wrinkle in Time*, or any of your other favorites, imagine that!
   b. Award-winning novels such as the *Harry Potter* series, *The Adventures of Huckleberry Finn*, *A Wrinkle in Time*, or any of your other favorites are imaginative.
   c. Imagine not being able to read such award-winning novels as the books in the *Harry Potter* series, *The Adventures of Huckleberry Finn*, *A Wrinkle in Time*, or any of your other favorites.
   d. If you couldn't read award-winning novels or your favorites, imagine what it would be like.

8. What is the **best** change, if any, to make in the sentence in lines 8–9 (*To be . . . we chose.*)?

   a. Change *effective* to **affective**.
   b. Insert a comma after **battle**.
   c. Change *chose* to **choose**.
   d. Make no change.

9. Which of the following is the **best** supporting detail to add after the sentence in line 19 (*Some topics . . . with others.*)?

   a. Television is just as healthy as reading, if not more so.
   b. If you want to read a copy of the Bill of Rights, you can visit the local library.
   c. Censors limit our freedoms many times, which makes life in America difficult.
   d. Authors sometimes intend to teach and familiarize people with unknown or uncomfortable topics.

10. What is the **best** change, if any, to make in the sentence in lines 28–31 (*Nancy Kranich . . . express themselves.*)?

    a. Change *themselves* to **herself**.
    b. Change *"each* to **"Each**.
    c. Remove the comma after **2000–2001**.
    d. Make no change.

TONY HAWK

Dena is in the seventh grade. She and the students in her English class have been asked to choose one person whom they admire and to write biographies of those persons. Dena must include reasons why the person she chooses is admirable. She writes a web of ideas, researches her topic, and writes her rough draft. She needs your help editing and revising it.

Here is Dena's rough draft. Read it and then answer questions 1–10.

1 No one could have known back in the 1970s that a hyperactive, nine-year-old
2 nuisance would become the world's best skater. When Tony Hawk first encountered
3 a skateboard a gift from his older brother his restless ways would be replaced with a
4 serene calm. Not only would he go on to become the best skater; he would also use
5 his experience to help other kids who were suffering from the same frustrations to
6 become involved in the sport.

7 Tony Hawk was born on May 12, 1968, in San Diego, California. Even at the
8 young age of six, Tony was determined to challenge himself beyond his abilities.
9 However, he would become so frustrated if he could not meet this challenge that he
10 would become depressed. His parents grew worried about they're son's behavior and
11 decided to have him psychologically evaluated. "The psychologist said he had a 12-
12 year-old mind in an 8-year-old body. And his mind tells him he can do things his body
13 can't do" his mother, Nancy, remembers.

14 When Tony's brother gave him his first skateboard, a thin Bahne board, things
15 seemed to balance out within his brain. Tony found the satisfaction he had been
16 looking for and grew calm. "He started thinking about other people and became more
17 generous," his brother recalls.

18 Nevertheless, Tony was still challenging himself. If he won a skateboarding
19 contest but felt that he hadn't skated his best, he would grow very upset. "If I don't
20 do my best, it kills me," he said.

21 Tony's father, Frank, encouraged him to pursue skating. He drove Tony up and
22 down the coast of California to compete in skating contests and built him a number
23 of skate ramps. Frank also founded the California Amateur Skateboard League and
24 the national skateboard association because he was dissatisfied with the
25 organizations that were then holding contests.

26 Tony received a sponsorship offer from Dogtown skateboards at the age of 12 and
27 he went pro just two years later. By the age of 16, he was the best skater in the
28 world. A year later, he bought his first house; this was followed by the purchase of
29 another when he was just 19 years old. Of course, he built skate ramps on his
30 property. He married Cindy Dunbar in April 1990.

31 Just a year later, in 1991, the popularity of skateboarding took a nosedive. Tony
32 found his income drying up and Cindy was soon supporting the family. Tony sold one

(continued on next page)

(continued from previous page)

```
33  of his homes, as well as many of the other luxury items purchased over the years.  In
34  1992, the couple's first son, Riley, was born and Tony started Birdhouse Projects, a
35  skateboard company with another pro skater, Per Welinder.

36      Fortunately, skateboarding gained in popularity once again and Tony was back on
37  top.  He married his current wife, Erin, in 1996.  Birdhouse is now one of the world's
38  largest skateboarding companies.  Tony started a clothing company, which was than
39  bought by Quiksilver in 2000.  He also created Tony Hawk's Pro Skater video games,
40  which have been bestsellers since they were first released.  He wrote a bestselling
41  autobiography, Hawk – Occupation: skateboarder, and created Tony Hawk's Gigantic
42  Skatepark Tour for ESPN.

43      Tony Hawk retired at the age of 31, when he stopped competitive skating.  He
44  founded the Tony Hawk Foundation, a non-profit organization that helps to bring
45  skateparks to low-income areas.  Tony believes that skateboarding kept it out of
46  trouble and away from the television.  Tony also operates the Boom Boom HuckJam
47  national arena tour, which features the world's best BMX bike riders, Motocross
48  riders, and skateboarders.  It consistently sells out at arenas in the twenty-four cities
49  that host it.
```

1. What is the **best** change, if any, to make in the sentence in lines 23–25 (*Frank also . . . holding contests.*)?

   a. Change *he* to **him**.
   b. Change *dissatisfied* to **disatisfied**.
   c. Change *national skateboard association* to **National Skateboard Association**.
   d. Make no change.

2. Which of the following is the **best** supporting detail to add after the sentence in lines 33–35 (*In 1992 . . . Per Welinder.*)?

   a. Many people gathered in the early 1990s to watch Tony skate.
   b. Tony found immediate success with his new company because the skateboarding industry was doing so well.
   c. Riley was Tony's business partner.
   d. However, the company did poorly at first and, two years after it was founded, Tony and Cindy divorced.

3. What is the **best** change, if any, to make in the sentence in lines 10–11 (*His parents . . . psychologically evaluated.*)?

   a. Change *they're* to **their**.
   b. Change *him* to **them**.
   c. Change *son's* to **sons'**.
   d. Make no change.

4. The sentence in lines 2–4 (*When Tony . . . serene calm.*) is poorly written. Which one of these is the **best** way to rewrite it?

   a. When Tony Hawk first, encountered a skateboard a gift from his older brother, his restless ways would be replaced with a serene calm.
   b. When Tony Hawk first encountered a skateboard a gift from his older brother, his restless ways, would be replaced with a serene calm.
   c. When Tony Hawk first encountered a skateboard, a gift from his older brother his restless ways would be replaced, with a serene calm.
   d. When Tony Hawk first encountered a skateboard, a gift from his older brother, his restless ways would be replaced with a serene calm.

5. What is the **best** change, if any, to make in the sentence in lines 12–13 (*And his . . . Nancy, remembers.*)?

   a. Remove the comma after **Nancy**.
   b. Insert a comma after **can't do**.
   c. Change *tells* to **had told**.
   d. Make no change.

6. What is the **best** change, if any, to make in the sentence in lines 45–46 (*Tony believes . . . the television.*)?

   a. Change *believes* to **beleives**.
   b. Change *it* to **him**.
   c. Insert a comma after **trouble**.
   d. Make no change.

7. Which transition would **best** fit at the beginning of the sentence in lines 31–32 (*Tony found . . . the family.*)?

   a. Suddenly,
   b. For example,
   c. However,
   d. Regardless,

8. What is the **best** change, if any, to make in the sentence in lines 38–39 (*Tony started . . . in 2000.*)?

   a. Change *Quiksilver* to **quiksilver**.
   b. Remove the comma after **company**.
   c. Change *than* to **then**.
   d. Make no change.

9. Dena wants to add the following sentence to the last paragraph: *He wants to offer that experience to other kids who may not be as fortunate as he was to have a family so supportive of his interest.* The sentence would **best** fit

   a. after the sentence in lines 48–49 (*It consistently . . . host it.*).
   b. after the sentence in lines 46–48 (*Tony also . . . and skateboarders.*).
   c. after the sentence in lines 45–46 (*Tony believes . . . the television.*).
   d. after the sentence in line 43 (*Tony Hawk . . . competitive skating.*).

10. What is the **best** change, if any, to make in the sentence in lines 33–35 (*In 1992 . . . Per Welinder.*)?

    a. Change *Birdhouse Projects* to **birdhouse projects**.
    b. Insert a comma after **company**.
    c. Remove the comma after **Riley**.
    d. Make no change.

BRIDGES

Caitlin's seventh-grade industrial arts class has been studying architecture and engineering. Her teacher has asked each student to write a report about a common architectural structure and describe what makes it successful. Caitlin visits the local library and researches her ideas. She has written her rough draft and needs your help editing and revising it.

Here is Caitlin's rough draft. Read it and then answer questions 1–10.

1   Whether you're driving down the road, hiking a nature trail, or riding a train
2 across the country, you will undoubtedly encounter one architectural marvel time
3 and again: the bridge. A bridge allows passage over some kind of obstacle, such as a
4 river, a valley, a road, or anything that needs crossing over! There are three major
5 types of bridges, the beam, arch, and suspension bridge. Most often, the type of
6 bridge built is determined by what obstacle needs to be crossed over.

7   Bridge types differ based on how far they stretch over a single space, or a "span."
8 A span is the distance between two bridge supports. A beam bridge can span a
9 distance of up to 200 feet. An arch bridge safely spans 800–1,000 feet. A suspension
10 bridge has the furthest span—7,000 feet? Whatever the type, the bridge must be able
11 to carry a heavy load without buckling or snapping.

12   The beam bridge is a stiff horizontal structure that rests on two columns. These
13 columns support the weight of the bridge and any traffic on it. These bridges were
14 used a lot during the Industrial Revolution. The size and height of the bridge control
15 the distance that the beam bridge can span. If a bridge designer needs the bridge to
16 be very tall, he must add a "truss" or a supporting web, to the horizontal beam. The
17 truss adds support to the bridge and makes it able to bear more weight.

18   The arch bridge is a semicircular structure with thick abutments. The weight
19 transfers to these abutments, making the arch bridge one of the strongest designs.
20 The arch bridge was a common design choice a long time ago. Many ancient Roman
21 arch bridges are still standing today. Similar to the beam bridge, the size and height
22 of the arch will limit the distance this bridge can reach.

23   The suspension bridge uses cables, ropes, or chains that are strung across the
24 obstacle being crossed. The deck of the bridge is then suspended from these cables.
25 Modern suspension bridges, which can be found around the world, have two tall
26 towers through which the cables are strung. The towers, which are dug deep into the
27 earth, support the weight of the bridge. Similar to the beam bridge, many suspension
28 bridges have a backup support system—the "truss." The truss in a suspension bridge
29 acts to keep the bridge from moving. There are two types of suspension bridges: the
30 "M" shape, featured in bridges like the golden gate bridge in San Francisco, and the
31 "A" shape, which is less common, but becoming more popular. An example of an "A"
32 shape suspension bridge can be seen in Boston.

(continued on next page)

(continued from previous page)

> 33   No matter how well-designed and well-built a bridge is, two main forces still can
> 34 destroy it. Resonance and weather. "Resonance" is a vibration that travels through
> 35 a bridge like a wave. In 1940, 40-mile-per-hour winds created resonance waves that
> 36 destroyed the Tacoma Narrows Bridge. The wind was hitting the bridge in just such
> 37 a manner that the bridge started vibrating. The resonance waves grew so large that
> 38 the bridge eventually broke apart. Another example of resonance would be the
> 39 vibration caused when a troop of soldiers march across a bridge. A large army that
> 40 doesn't break the rhythm of their marching when traveling over a bridge could
> 41 destroy the bridge.
>
> 42   Weather is unpredictable and uncontrollable. While new bridge designs try to
> 43 compensate for the effects of rain, ice, wind, and salt, weather-related damages
> 44 account for more bridge disasters than do design flaws. Only preventative
> 45 maintinence can be helpful.

1. Where is there an incomplete sentence?

   a. in lines 20–21 (*Many ancient . . . standing today.*)
   b. in line 8 (*A span . . . bridge supports.*)
   c. in lines 3–4 (*A bridge . . . crossing over!*)
   d. in line 34 (*Resonance . . . weather.*)

2. What is the **best** change, if any, to make in the sentence in lines 9–10 (*A suspension . . . 7,000 feet?*)?

   a. Change *furthest* to **farthest**.
   b. Change the *question mark* to an **exclamation point**.
   c. Change *has* to **have**.
   d. Make no change.

3. What would be the **best** way to rewrite the sentence in line 20 (*The arch . . . time ago.*) to make it more specific?

   a. The arch bridge was a common design choice when people were looking for something sturdy.
   b. The arch bridge was a common design choice during the Roman, Baroque, and Renaissance periods.
   c. The arch bridge was a common design choice before there were cars and people liked them better, anyway.
   d. The arch bridge was a common design choice in places where they needed to cross over something.

4. What is the **best** change, if any, to make in the sentence in lines 29–31 (*There are . . . more popular.*)?

   a. Change *golden gate bridge* to **Golden Gate Bridge**.
   b. Remove the comma after **"A" shape**.
   c. Remove the comma after **Francisco**.
   d. Make no change.

5. Which of the following is the **best** supporting detail to add after the sentence in lines 13–14 (*These bridges . . . Industrial Revolution.*)?

   a. A beam bridge spans distances of up to 200 feet.
   b. During the Industrial Revolution, these bridges were fairly common.
   c. Beam bridges are similar to arch and suspension bridges.
   d. Today, beam bridges can commonly be found on highway overpasses.

6. What is the **best** way to rewrite the sentence in lines 39–41 (*A large . . . the bridge.*) to improve the paragraph?

   a. A large army that doesn't rhythmically march over a destroyed bridge can travel over the bridge.
   b. The bridge the large army travels over makes them march rhythmically.
   c. A large army that doesn't break the rhythm of their marching when traveling over a bridge could destroy it.
   d. Rhythmic marching could destroy a bridge, so a large army doesn't break it.

7. What is the **best** change, if any, to make in the sentence in lines 44–45 (*Only preventative . . . be helpful.*)?

   a. Change *be* to **have been**.
   b. Change *maintinence* to **maintenance**.
   c. Change the *period* to a **question mark**.
   d. Make no change.

8. What is the **best** change, if any, to make in the sentence in lines 15–16 (*If a . . . horizontal beam.*)?

   a. Insert a comma after **"truss**.
   b. Change *horizontal* to **horisontal**.
   c. Change *he* to **him**.
   d. Make no change.

9. The sentence in lines 4–5 (*There are . . . suspension bridge.*) is poorly written. Which one of these is the **best** way to rewrite it?

   a. There are three major types of beam, arch, and suspension bridges.
   b. There are beam, arch, and suspension bridges, three major types.
   c. There are three major types: the beam, the arch, and the suspension bridge.
   d. There are three major types of bridges, the beam bridge, the arch bridge, and the suspension bridge.

10. Caitlin wants to add the following sentence to the fourth paragraph: *Arches made of stone, in fact, don't even need any mortar to hold the stones together.* The sentence would **best** fit

    a. after the sentence in line 18 (*The arch . . . thick abutments.*).
    b. after the sentence in lines 18–19 (*The weight . . . strongest designs.*).
    c. after the sentence in lines 20–21 (*Many ancient . . . standing today.*).
    d. after the sentence in lines 21–22 (*Similar to . . . can reach.*).

Air Racing

Jan's seventh-grade history class has been studying how technology unites foreign countries. His teacher has asked that each student write about a topic of his or her choosing that would illustrate this idea. Jan chooses his topic and writes his rough draft. He needs your help editing and revising it.

Here is Jan's rough draft. Read it and then answer questions 1–10.

1   The first air race was held in Rheims, France, in August 1909, just six years after
2   the Wright brothers's first flight. Spectators, some of whom had never seen an airplane
3   before, gathered to watch the pilots compete for prizes. An American, Glenn H. Curtiss,
4   won the two biggest prizes: the James Gordon Bennett Trophy for the fastest two laps
5   and the *Prix de la Vitesse* for the fastest three laps. Air racing was born.

6   The first United States air race was held in Los Angeles less than a year later.
7   Curtiss set a record of 55 miles per hour for a plane with one passenger. In October
8   1910, the second international meet was held in Elmont, New York. The Bennett
9   Trophy race attracted dozens of planes and pilots from Europe and the United States.
10 During World War I, Bennett Trophy racing was suspended. Many races were
11 postponed until the war ended. In 1920, the French won their third consecutive
12 Bennett Trophy, thus retiring the trophy and ending this competition.

13 Other trophies were offered to the best air race pilots. The Michelin Cup was
14 awarded for the longest flight between sunrise and sundown on a single day. Orville
15 Wright won the first competition for this trophy in 1908. The *London Daily Mail*
16 prize was awarded for the first flight over the English channel. In 1909, Louis
17 Bleriot of France won it. After World War I, in 1919, two British military pilots won
18 the £10,000 prize for flying nonstop between England and America. The Jacques
19 Schneider Trophy was initiated in 1913, and was for seaplane races over open water.
20 It, too, was suspended during World War I, but resumed following the war. The
21 $25,000 prize offered, in 1919, by a New York hotel owner for a nonstop flight
22 between New York and France would ultimately led to the famous Charles Lindbergh
23 flight. Lindbergh claimed this prize in 1927.

24 The Pulitzer Trophy for international air races held in America was announced in
25 1919. The first race was held in 1920 on Long Island. Charles Moseley took home
26 the trophy for averaging 156.5 miles per hour over a closed-circuit course. As many
27 as 25,000 spectators gathered to watch. In 1921, a national air meet was established.
28 It later became known as the National Air Races.

29 The John L. Mitchell Trophy meets, begun in 1924, were the first air races to set
30 planes against other planes on a closed-circuit course. These races were very
31 popular among spectators. By 1929, there were 27 similar closed-circuit events at
32 the National Air Races. One of these events was the Women's Air Derby, which
33 began on August 13th in California and ended on August 20th in Cleveland. Among
34 the twenty competitors was Amelia Earhart. This event led to the establishment of

(continued on next page)

(continued from previous page)

35 the All-Woman Transcontinental Air Race, or what was called the "Powder Puff
36 Derby," after World War II.

37   The Great Depression took its toll on air racing and attendance numbers declined
38 during the 1930s. Nevertheless, the National Air Races continued until 1939. With
39 the importance of airplanes in World War II the popularity of air races grew once
40 again. The National Air Races started up in 1946 in Cleveland. This time, they were
41 sponsored by the War Department. In 1949, an accident occurred when a prop plane
42 crashed into a house. The pilot and a mother and her child were all killed. The
43 National Air Races became stunted for a time.

44   But air racing would not die. The National Air Show began in 1951 and involved
45 primarily military planes. The Defense Department ruled in 1957 that military
46 aircraft could no longer take part in the contest so the National Air Show was
47 discontinued. Some people's passion for racing kept the sport alive. They formed
48 what would become the National Air-Racing Group; this existed until 1964 when
49 Reno revived the National Air Races as part of the centennial celebration of Nevada's
50 statehood. Drawing hundreds of thousands of fans from around the world, the
51 competition still goes on today.

1. What is the **best** change, if any, to make in the sentence in lines 38–40 (*With the . . . once again.*)?

   a. Change *air races* to **Air Races**.
   b. Change *grew* to **had grown**.
   c. Insert a comma after **II**.
   d. Make no change.

2. Which of the following is the **best** supporting detail to add after the sentence in lines 11–12 (*In 1920 . . . this competition.*)?

   a. There may or may not have been Swedish pilots in this race.
   b. The Bennett Trophy had already been won by an American.
   c. Although the French had won many trophies, the fact that they had never won the Bennett Trophy truly aggravated them.
   d. Frenchman Jules Vedrines, who won the trophy in 1912, was the first pilot to average more than 100 miles per hour.

3. What is the **best** change, if any, to make in the sentence in lines 20–23 (*The $25,000 . . . Lindbergh flight.*)?

   a. Change *hotel owner* to **Hotel Owner**.
   b. Change *led* to **lead**.
   c. Change *ultimately* to **ultimatly**.
   d. Make no change.

4. The sentence in lines 45–47 (*The Defense . . . was discontinued.*) is poorly written. Which one of these is the **best** way to rewrite it?

   a. In 1957, when the Defense Department ruled that military aircraft could no longer take part in the contest, the National Air Show was discontinued.
   b. The National Air Show ruled that military aircraft could no longer take part in the contest in 1957, so the Defense Department was discontinued.
   c. The National Department, in 1957, ruled that the Defense Air Show could no longer include military aircraft and, thus, it should be discontinued.
   d. The Defense Department could no longer allow military aircraft in the contest, so the National Air Show was discontinued, in 1957.

5. What is the **best** change, if any, to make in the sentence in lines 15–16 (*The London . . . English channel.*)?

   a. Insert a comma after **flight**.
   b. Change *channel* to **Channel**.
   c. Change *was* to **is**.
   d. Make no change.

6. Jan wants to add the following sentence to the last paragraph: *Many were former fighter pilots who had bought war surplus planes, civilians who had built their own small planes, or antique aircraft enthusiasts who owned old biplanes.* The sentence would **best** fit

   a. after the sentence in lines 44–45 (*The National . . . military planes.*).
   b. after the sentence in line 47 (*Some people's . . . sport alive.*).
   c. after the sentence in lines 47–50 (*They formed . . . Nevada's statehood.*).
   d. after the sentence in lines 50–51 (*Drawing hundreds . . . on today.*).

7. What is the **best** change, if any, to make in the sentence in lines 1–2 (*The first . . . first flight.*)?

    a. Change *brothers's* to **brothers'**.
    b. Insert a comma after **August**.
    c. Remove the comma after **Rheims**.
    d. Make no change.

8. Which transition would **best** fit at the beginning of the sentence in lines 10–11 (*Many races . . . war ended.*)?

    a. However,
    b. Nevertheless,
    c. For instance,
    d. In fact,

9. What is the **best** change, if any, to make in the sentence in lines 33–34 (*Among the . . . Amelia Earhart.*)?

    a. Change *twenty* to **twentey**.
    b. Change *Among* to **Amoung**.
    c. Change *competiters* to **competitors**.
    d. Make no change.

10. The sentence in lines 18–19 (*The Jacques . . . open water.*) is poorly written. Which one of these is the **best** way to rewrite it?

    a. The Jacques Schneider Trophy, initiated in 1913, was for seaplane races over open water.
    b. The Jacques Schneider Trophy was for seaplane races over open water, initiated in 1913.
    c. In 1913, the Jacques Schneider Trophy was for seaplane races initiated over open water.
    d. The seaplane races over open water, in 1913, were awarded the Jacques Schneider Trophy.

An American Symbol

Krystal's seventh-grade social studies class has recently been looking at symbols that characterize American style and traditions. Her teacher asks the students to write reports describing objects of some kind that are commonly tied to United States culture. Krystal has spent some time at the local library and written her report. She needs your help editing and revising it.

Here is Krystal's rough draft. Read it and then answer questions 1–10.

1 Converse™ sneakers are a symbol of American culture and tradition. They have
2 been used in sports and for casaul wear for almost a century. The company offers
3 several footwear and clothing for sports performance, sports classics, and sports
4 lifestyle for men, women, and children.

5 Converse was established by Marquis M. Converse in 1908. The company calls
6 itself "America's Original Sports Company." Their shoes have been tied to such
7 sports as basketball, tennis turf, and track. The Converse All Star®, introduced in
8 1917, was the world's first performance basketball shoe.

9 Basketball, which derived from the Converse All Star, was revolutionized by the
10 Chuck Taylor® All Star. It was commonly worn among basketball players, around
11 the world for almost fifty years. "Chucks," Cons," or "Connies," as they have been
12 called, were first introduced in 1923. To date, more than 750 million pairs have been
13 sold in 144 countries.

14 For much of the twentieth century, Converse shoes were dominant on the
15 basketball court. Legends such as Julius Erving ("Dr. J"), an amazing talent from
16 the 1970s, made the Pro Leather, Pro Star, and Weapon™ basketball shoes popular.
17 The new designs of the shoes offered an opportunity to gain speed and agility, while
18 exhibited creativity and self-expression. Converse still provides basketball footwear
19 today.

20 Converse shoes can be found far off the basketball court, too. They have become
21 a common trend among Americas youth, who are often drawn to their original,
22 unique look and creative designs. The Jack Purcell® shoe, named for a famous
23 badminton champion, came on the scene in 1935 with the well-known Smile™ on the
24 front. The Converse One Star® is popular in the surf and skate community.

25 Converse shoes have always characterized creativity and self-expression. Many
26 Americans value these traits. People can often gain an impression of someone just
27 by seeing how him or her is dressed. Converse offers footwear and clothing for
28 unique, creative people who want to make a bold statement. What better expression
29 of United States culture is there?

1. What is the **best** change, if any, to make in the sentence in lines 6–7 (*Their shoes . . . and track.*)?

   a. Change *basketball, tennis turf, and track* to **Basketball, Tennis Turf, and Track**.
   b. Change *have* to **has**.
   c. Insert a comma after **tennis**.
   d. Make no change.

2. What is the **best** change, if any, to make in the sentence in lines 10–11 (*It was . . . fifty years.*)?

   a. Change *fifty* to **fiftey**.
   b. Remove the comma after **players**.
   c. Change *world* to **World**.
   d. Make no change.

3. What is the **best** change, if any, to make in the sentence in lines 26–27 (*People can . . . is dressed.*)?

   a. Change *is* to **are**.
   b. Change *him or her* to **he or she**.
   c. Change *impression* to **empression**.
   d. Make no change.

4. The sentence in lines 2–4 (*The company . . . and children.*) is poorly written. Which one of these is the **best** way to rewrite it?

   a. The company offers collections of men's, women's, and children's footwear and clothing for sports performance, classics, and lifestyle.
   b. Men, women, and children can get several kinds of footwear and clothing from the company for sports performance and sports lifestyle.
   c. Several of footwears and clothings from the company can be had for men, women, and children for sports performance, sports classics, and sports lifestyle.
   d. Sports performance, sports classics, and sports lifestyle are offered by the company. They are available for men and women.

5. What is the **best** change, if any, to make in the sentence in lines 11–12 (*"Chucks," Cons."... in 1923.*)?

   a. Remove the comma after **called**.
   b. Insert a comma after **introduced**.
   c. Insert quotation marks before **Cons,"**.
   d. Make no change.

6. Krystal wants to add the following sentence to the fifth paragraph: *These shoes were popular in early Hollywood and among boarding-school "bad boys."* The sentence would **best** fit

   a. after the sentence in line 20 (*Converse shoes ... court, too.*).
   b. after the sentence in lines 20–22 (*They have ... creative designs.*).
   c. after the sentence in lines 22–24 (*The Jack ... the front.*).
   d. after the sentence in line 24 (*The Converse ... skate community.*).

7. What is the **best** change, if any, to make in the sentence in lines 1–2 (*They have ... a century.*)?

   a. Change *casaul* to **casual**.
   b. Insert a comma after **sports**.
   c. Change *They* to **Them**.
   d. Make no change.

8. What is the **best** change, if any, to make in the sentence in lines 20–22 (*They have ... creative designs.*)?

   a. Change *their* to **they're**.
   b. Remove the comma after **original**.
   c. Change *Americas* to **America's**.
   d. Make no change.

9. What is the **best** change, if any, to make in the sentence in lines 17–18 (*The new ... and self-expression.*)?

   a. Change *opportunity* to **oportunity**.
   b. Insert a comma after **shoes**.
   c. Change *exhibited* to **exhibiting**.
   d. Make no change.

10. The sentence in lines 9–10 (*Basketball, which . . . All Star.*) is poorly written. Which one of these is the **best** way to rewrite it?

    a. The Chuck Taylor® All Star, which derived from the Converse All Star, was revolutionized by basketball.
    b. The Chuck Taylor® All Star was revolutionized by basketball, which derived from the Converse All Star.
    c. The Converse All Star revolutionized basketball, and derived from the Chuck Taylor® All Star.
    d. The Chuck Taylor® All Star, which derived from the Converse All Star, revolutionized basketball.

MAGNETIC MAGIC

Grover's assignment for his seventh-grade science class is to choose a toy that he remembers playing with when he was younger and write a report about how scientific principles relate to it. Grover selects his favorite childhood toy, researches how it works, and writes a rough draft. He needs your help editing and revising it.

Here is Grover's rough draft. Read it and then answer questions 1–10.

1 In 1974, four engineers at the pilot pen corporation invented one of the most
2 popular drawing toys. Today, more than 40 million have sold. The invention was the
3 Magna Doodle™. The Magna Doodle is not only a fun, creative toy; it is also a
4 scientific study of magnitizm.

5 The basic Magna Doodle is made up of several parts: a white, plastic screen on
6 which to draw; a pen with a magnet at the tip that is attached by a string; a magnet
7 that works to erase the screen; and the case in which the mechanism is contained.
8 These parts all work together to create a "dustless chalkboard" that has been used by
9 underwater divers, coaches, and teachers, as well as on road trips and in the home.
10 There is less mess and less waste in using the Magna Doodle instead of paper or
11 traditional chalkboards.

12 The white, plastic screen is technically called a "magnetophoretic display panel.
13 It is made up of three layers. The front and back are pieces of transparent or semi-
14 transparent plastic. The middle is a honeycombed or hexagonal plastic web. Each
15 cell of the web is filled with a thick liquid substance that contains many tiny
16 magnetic particles. The pen and eraser pull the dark, small, fine particles around to
17 create (or erase) drawings and writing.

18 The magnetic pen has a small magnet at the tip, which is strong enough to pull
19 the particles through the liquid. The liquid is thick. The magnetic particles are
20 prevented from sinking because of this, so what is drawn can be seen over time.
21 White dye is mixed into the liquid to provide a contrast between the particles and the
22 liquid. This is why the drawing is so easy to see.

23 The eraser is actually a bar magnet that slides back and forth to pull the magnetic
24 particles, from the front of the magnetophoretic display to the back. It seem to
25 magically disappear! They are nearly invisible behind the thick liquid. They are also
26 being held to the back of the display until the magnetic pen is used pulling them to
27 the front.

28 It is amazing that a child's toy could be so intricate. There are so many things
29 going on to make my drawings appear and reappear. Science aside, however, the
30 Magna Doodle is just a really fun toy to play with!

1. What is the **best** change, if any, to make in the sentence in lines 23–24 (*The eraser . . . the back.*)?

   a. Change *to pull* to **pulled**.
   b. Insert a comma after **display**.
   c. Remove the comma after **particles**.
   d. Make no change.

2. What is the **best** change, if any, to make in the sentence in lines 1–2 (*In 1974 . . . drawing toys.*)?

   a. Change *most popular* to **popularest**.
   b. Change *pilot pen corporation* to **Pilot Pen Corporation**.
   c. Insert a comma after **engineers**.
   d. Make no change.

3. What is the **best** change, if any, to make in the sentence in lines 16–17 (*The pen . . . and writing.*)?

   a. Insert a comma after **create**.
   b. Remove the comma after **small**.
   c. Change *create* to **creates**.
   d. Make no change.

4. Which of the following is the **best** way to combine the two sentences in lines 19–20 (*The liquid . . . over time.*)?

   a. The thickness of the liquid prevents the magnetic particles from sinking, so that what is drawn can be seen over time.
   b. What is drawn can be seen over time, which prevents the magnetic particles from sinking in the thick liquid.
   c. Over time, the thick liquid prevents the magnetic particles from sinking, so what is drawn can be seen over time.
   d. The magnetic particles, from sinking in the thick liquid, so what can be seen over time is drawn.

5. What is the **best** change, if any, to make in the sentence in lines 3–4 (*The Magna . . . of magnitizm.*)?

   a. Change *is not* to **was not**.
   b. Change *magnitizm* to **magnetism**.
   c. Insert a comma after **scientific**.
   d. Make no change.

6. What is the **best** change, if any, to make in the sentence in lines 24–25 (*It seem . . . magically disappear!*)?

   a. Change *to* to **too**.
   b. Change the *exclamation point* to a **period**.
   c. Change *seem* to **seems**.
   d. Make no change.

7. Which transition would best fit at the beginning of the sentence in line 25 (*They are . . . thick liquid.*)?

   a. However,
   b. For example,
   c. In fact,
   d. Moreover,

8. The sentence in lines 10–11 (*There is . . . traditional chalkboards.*) is poorly written. Which one of these is the **best** way to rewrite it?

   a. Traditional chalkboards and paper create less mess and less waste than the Magna Doodle.
   b. Less mess and less waste are created by using Magna Doodle instead of paper or traditional chalkboards, both of which create a big mess and a lot of waste.
   c. The Magna Doodle uses paper and traditional chalkboards to make less mess and less waste.
   d. Using the Magna Doodle instead of paper or traditional chalkboards creates less mess and less waste.

9. What is the **best** change, if any, to make in the sentence in lines 25–27 (*They are . . . the front.*)?

    a. Change *pulling* to **to pull**.
    b. Insert a comma after **display**.
    c. Change the *period* to a **question mark**.
    d. Make no change.

10. What is the **best** change, if any, to make in the sentence in line 12 (*The white . . . display panel.*)?

    a. Insert a comma after **a**.
    b. Change *magnetophoretic* to **Magnetophoretic**.
    c. Insert quotation marks after **panel.**
    d. Make no change.

MARGARET ATWOOD   49

Karina's seventh-grade English teacher selects one student every three weeks to write a report on a poet of his or her choosing. It is Karina's turn. Since she wants to be a poet herself, Karina enthusiastically begins her research. She has written her rough draft, but needs your help editing and revising it.

Here is Karina's rough draft. Read it and then answer questions 1–10.

1   Margaret Atwood is among the world's most prolific female writers of the past one
2   hundred years. Margaret was born on November 18, 1939, in Ottawa Canada. This
3   was nearly three months before the advent of World War II. As early as May 1940,
4   her father, who was doing research as a forest entomologist, took her to the forest of
5   northwestern Quebec. Her parents were unconventional for the time. They avoided
6   civilization and did not strive to become the everyday 1940s household. As a result,
7   Margaret spent much of her young life in the woods and by herself. She learned to
8   read early on and spent much of her time reading anything she could find.

9   Margaret created her first poetry book at the age of five. It held all the poems she
10 could remember. It had nursery rhymes and some of her own first original works at
11 the end. She would not write again for another eleven years. At the age of sixteen,
12 the year being 1956, Margaret was in her fourth year of high school in Toronto. She
13 crossed the football field on her way home from school when, as she described it, "a
14 large invisible thumb descended from the sky and pressed down on the top of my
15 head. A poem formed. It was quite a gloomy poem: the poems of the young usually
16 are. It was a gift, this poem, . . . both exciting and sinister at the same time."

17 Margaret said that her ignorance of any poetry written after the year 1900 meant
18 that she had virtually no knowledge of free verse. Her first "real" poem rhymed and
19 was filled with dark themes, such as those she had read in Lord Byron or Edgar Allen
20 Poe's works. Nevertheless, she contends that on that day in 1956, she officially
21 became a poet. Her former English teacher, who were studying the author's life, told
22 some documentary filmmakers that Margaret had shown no particular promise in
23 her class. No doubt she was surprised to find that Margaret would later become one
24 of the most famous female poets of all time.

25 Of course, Margaret does admit that she as a poet remained ignorant for a good
26 many years after that day as well. While no one told her outright that she couldn't
27 be a poet, most people in 1950s Canada considered an occupation as a writer to be
28 absurd. When her twelfth-grade English teacher, Miss Bessie Billings, finally read
29 her poetry, Margaret received this response: "I can't understand a word of this, dear,
30 so it must be good." This brief word of encouragement was more then she had ever
31 received.

32 After working in journalism and studying English literature (where she finally
33 realized that not all poetry had to rhyme), Margaret began publishing in small
34 magazines and writing reviews. She put together a collection of poems for

(continued on next page)

(continued from previous page)

35 publication. But was rejected time and time again. While she knew that her poetry
36 was getting better, she also knew she could not make a living at it unless she took a
37 more active role. She decided to self-publish a collection of her work. Today, those
38 small booklets are worth over $1,800 each.

39   Several years went by and Margaret began teaching grammar to engineering
40 students in british columbia. She describes this time vividly: "I taught in the
41 daytime, ate canned food, [and] did not wash my dishes until all of them were dirty."
42 In that year, she also completed her first published book of poems, *The Circle Game*,
43 as well as her first published novel. The poetry book won the coveted Governor
44 General's Award.

45   She continues to write today, balancing writing novels and poetry, so that she
46 won't go "slowly down a long dark tunnel with no exit." Margaret Atwood always
47 finds that when she writes poetry, it still is as surprising and mysterious as when
48 that hand descended in 1956.

1. The sentence in lines 21–23 (*Her former . . . her class.*) is poorly written. Which one of these is the **best** way to rewrite it?

    a. Her former English teacher, who were studying the author's life, told some documentary filmmakers that the teacher had shown no particular promise in Margaret's class.
    b. Margaret had shown no particular promise in the class of her former English teacher, who were studying the author's life, she told some documentary filmmakers.
    c. Her former English teacher told some documentary filmmakers, who were studying the author's life, that Margaret had shown no particular promise in her class.
    d. Some documentary filmmakers told Margaret that she had shown no particular promise in her former English teacher's class.

2. What is the **best** change, if any, to make in the sentence in lines 30–31 (*This brief . . . ever received.*)?

    a. Change *then* to **than**.
    b. Change *received* to **recieved**.
    c. Change *she* to **her**.
    d. Make no change.

3. Karina wants to add the following sentence to the fifth paragraph: *She printed 250 copies and sold them for 50 cents each.* The sentence would **best** fit

    a. after the sentence in line 37 (*She decided . . . her work.*).
    b. after the sentence in lines 35–37 (*While she . . . active role.*).
    c. after the sentence in lines 34–35 (*She put . . . for publication.*).
    d. after the sentence in lines 32–34 (*After working . . . writing reviews.*).

4. What is the **best** change, if any, to make in the sentence in line 2 (*Margaret was . . . Ottawa Canada.*)?

    a. Remove the comma after **18**.
    b. Insert a comma after **Ottawa**.
    c. Change *was* to **were**.
    d. Make no change.

5. Which of the following is the **best** way to combine the two sentences in lines 9–11 (*It held . . . the end.*)?

    a. It had some of her own first original works and some nursery rhymes at the end.
    b. It held nursery rhymes and some of her own first original works, all the ones she could remember, anyway.
    c. It had all the poems she could remember and some of her own at the end.
    d. It held a collection of all the poems she could remember, such as nursery rhymes, with some of her own first original works at the end.

6. What is the **best** change, if any, to make in the sentence in lines 39–40 (*Several years . . . british columbia.*)?

    a. Change *grammar* to **grammer**.
    b. Insert a comma after **by**.
    c. Change *british columbia* to **British Columbia**.
    d. Make no change.

7. Where is there an incomplete sentence?

    a. in lines 23–24 (*No doubt . . . all time.*)
    b. in lines 28–30 (*When her . . . be good."*)
    c. in line 35 (*But was . . . time again.*)
    d. in lines 43–44 (*The poetry . . . General's Award.*)

8. What is the **best** change, if any, to make in the sentence in lines 12–15 (*She crossed . . . my head.*)?

   a. Change *crossed* to **was crossing**.
   b. Remove the comma after **when**.
   c. Change *football* to **Football**.
   d. Make no change.

9. What is the **best** way to rewrite the sentence in lines 7–8 (*She learned . . . could find.*) to improve the paragraph?

   a. She learned how to read early on, so she read a lot.
   b. She learned how to read early on and spent much of her time buried in any book she could find.
   c. She learned how to read early on and spent much of her time reading, almost as much time as she spent learning how to read.
   d. She learned how to read early on, so she read anything she could find.

10. The sentence in lines 46–48 (*Margaret Atwood . . . in 1956.*) is poorly written. Which one of these is the **best** way to rewrite it?

    a. She always is still surprising and mysterious as when that hand descended in 1956 whenever she writes poetry.
    b. Writing poetry still surprises and mystifies her like she writes it by hand.
    c. Margaret Atwood finds that writing poetry is still as surprising and mysterious as when that hand descended upon her in 1956.
    d. She always is surprised and mystified by writing poetry, just like when that hand descended in 1956 and surprised her.

CHICAGO'S MILLENNIUM PARK

Miles lives in Chicago, Illinois. Miles's seventh-grade class has recently taken a trip to the brand-new Millennium Park in Chicago. His history teacher asks each student to write a letter to a friend who hasn't visited the park, describing the features of the park and persuading that person to plan a trip. Miles makes a brief outline to map out his ideas and writes his rough draft. He needs your help editing and revising it.

Here is Miles's rough draft. Read it and then answer questions 1–10.

1   Dear Pedro,

2   I just got back from visiting the Millennium Park in Chicago and I had to write to
3   tell you about it. Pedro, it is incredible! You can see some incredible examples of
4   modern art there. I think it's going to draw tourists to the city for many, many years.

5   The park opened on July 16th and drew tens of thousands of people. Most of these
6   visitors probably remember what was there before: a railroad yard and a parking lot.
7   Now, the 24-acre park presents a beautiful view. As well as more money for the city.
8   It has a stainless-steel pavilion for concerts and a pedestrian bridge. Frank Gehry
9   designed them. The park also has a unique, reflective, teardrop-shaped sculpture by
10   Anish Kapoor. People are already calling it the "Bean"! The real name of the
11   sculpture is "Cloud Gate." It is sixty-six feet long and thirty-three feet high. People
12   were standing in front of it, waving, and taking pictures of themselves. It was to
13   funny.

14   The park also has Crown Fountain by Jaume Plensa. The little kids at the park
15   really liked this the best. It is a gigantic fountain with water cascading off two 50-
16   foot video screen towers. The screens shows pictures of Chicago and its residents.
17   About every five minutes or so, a gigantic face would shoot a stream of water out of
18   its mouth. The little kids would go crazy!

19   There is also a public theater, a bicycle station, a promenade, and an ice rink. One
20   of the best features of the park is Frank Gehry's Pritzker Pavilion, which offers the
21   most amazing acoustics in the city. Although it is close to heavy traffic areas like
22   Michigan avenue and Columbus drive, the sound in the pavilion cannot be muted.
23   For the most part, the orchestra, chorus, and solo singers could be heard clearly from
24   any point in the park. Almost 100 speakers hang 30 feet above the audience.
25   Overhead is a crisscross metal trellis of stainless steel. The sound produced was awe-
26   inspiring.

27   Its interesting that the park that was supposed to be launched at the dawn of the
28   millennium didn't actually open until 2004. It was also supposed to cost the city
29   about $150 million dollars, but by the time it was finished, it was up to $475 million
30   dollars. Some residents have complained that the amount of money spent on
31   building the park has hurt other local projects. Mayor Richard Daley doesn't seem

(continued on next page)

(continued from previous page)

> 32 to mind, though, as he sees Millennium Park as a centerpiece of his grand vision for
> 33 beautifying the city.
>
> 34   When you come back to Chicago, I'd love to take you to Millennium Park. I plan
> 35 on going many, many more times to enjoy all the new sights and sounds. I hope to
> 36 hear from you soon!
>
> 37   Your Friend,
>
> 38   Miles

1. What is the **best** change, if any, to make in the sentence in lines 12–13 (*It . . . funny.*)?

   a. Change *to* to **too**.
   b. Change the *period* to a **question mark**.
   c. Change *was* to **were**.
   d. Make no change.

2. Which of the following is the **best** supporting detail to add after the sentence in lines 23–24 (*For the . . . the park.*)?

   a. The pavilion was designed to feel like an enclosed space for the 4,000 people sitting in fixed seats and the 7,000 people sitting in the lawn area.
   b. The mayor was very excited about the new features of the park.
   c. Children who were playing in the fountain seemed to like the bicycle station and the ice rink, too.
   d. Whenever I come to the park, I get the feeling that I'm standing in a parking lot.

3. What is the **best** change, if any, to make in the sentence in line 16 (*The screens . . . its residents.*)?

   a. Change *its* to **it's**.
   b. Insert a comma after **Chicago**.
   c. Change *shows* to **show**.
   d. Make no change.

4. What is the **best** change, if any, to make in line 37 (*Your Friend,*)?

   a. Change *Your* to **You're**.
   b. Change *Friend* to **friend**.
   c. Remove the comma after **Friend**.
   d. Make no change.

5. What is the **best** way to rewrite the sentence in lines 3–4 (*You can . . . art there.*) to improve the paragraph?

   a. Modern art is there and you can see it if you go there.
   b. If you go there, you can see incredible examples of modern art.
   c. There, you can see incredible examples of modern art.
   d. You can see some remarkable examples of modern art there.

6. Miles wants to add the following sentence to the fifth paragraph in the body of his letter: *Almost half of that money was raised by private donations from wealthy Chicago families, and the rest came from the city and corporations.* The sentence would **best** fit

   a. after the sentence in lines 27–28 (*Its interesting . . . .until 2004.*).
   b. after the sentence in lines 28–30 (*It was . . . million dollars.*).
   c. after the sentence in lines 30–31 (*Some residents . . . local projects.*).
   d. after the sentence in lines 31–33 (*Mayor Richard . . . the city.*).

7. What is the **best** change, if any, to make in the sentence in lines 21–22 (*Although it . . . be muted.*)?

   a. Remove the comma after **drive**.
   b. Change *pavilion* to **Pavilion**.
   c. Change *avenue* and *drive* to **Avenue** and **Drive**.
   d. Make no change.

8. Where is there an incomplete sentence?

   a. in line 35–36 (*I hope . . . you soon!*)
   b. in line 24 (*Almost 100 . . . the audience.*)
   c. in line 18 (*The little . . . go crazy!*)
   d. in line 7 (*As well . . . the city.*)

9. What is the **best** change, if any, to make in the sentence in lines 27–28 (*Its interesting . . . until 2004.*)?

   a. Change *millennium* to **Millennium**.
   b. Change *Its* to **It's**.
   c. Insert a comma after **interesting**.
   d. Make no change.

10. What is the **best** way to rewrite the sentence in lines 28–30 (*It was . . . million dollars.*) to improve the paragraph?

   a. While the supposed cost of the project was about $150 million, the price had risen to $475 million by the time it was finished.
   b. It did cost $150 million dollars, but then it cost an additional $475, to build the park.
   c. The cost of the park was supposed to be about $150 million dollars, but the price went up to $475 million dollars eventually by the time it was finished.
   d. The park cost of $150 million dollars skyrocketed to $475 million dollars when it was finally finished.

A Message from the Future

Alexis's seventh-grade environmental science teacher gave the class the following writing prompt and asked them to write reports in response to it: *Imagine it is fifty years into the future. Think about how you might perceive the environmental problems in existence today. Write a letter to someone in the present time, telling him or her about what technology he or she could be using today to help to improve air quality in New York City.* Alexis has devised a web of ideas and has written her rough draft. She needs your help editing and revising it.

Here is Alexis's rough draft. Read it and then answer questions 1–10.

1   Dear Mr. Sellers,

2   If you're like most people, you probably drive a gas-powered car. You may be
3   aware of the toxins you are releasing into the environment, and the collective harm
4   caused by all of those cars, trucks, vans, and SUVs on the roadways. There are steps
5   you could take to improve the air quality around you. Have you ever thought about
6   traveling on air?

7   Gasoline is expensive, and when you consider all of the harm it does to the
8   environment, you should be seeking alternatives. Furthermore, gasoline will at some
9   point disappear altogether, so people must have an alternative means of getting
10 around. One not so dependent upon this non-renewable resource. In your lifetime,
11 hybrid cars have become an option. Alternative engines power these vehicles. These
12 include electric and fuel-cell-powered types of engines.

13   Consider the e.Volution car, an air-powered vehicle introduced by Zero Pollution
14 Motors in Brignoles France. The exhaust from the e.Volution's engine will not
15 contain pollutants. The compressed air that fuels the car lasts for up to 124 miles
16 and reaches speeds as high as 60 miles per hour. Instead of refueling at the gas
17 pump, however, you can just fill up at the most near air pump! Furthermore, you
18 would only have to change the oil every 31,000 miles, instead of every 3,000 like most
19 of your modern-day vehicles.

20   Not long after the news broke about this revolutionary new technology, the
21 Mexican government signed a deal to buy 40,000 e.Volutions to use as taxis. (Mexico
22 City is extremely polluted.) Due to the fact that the e.Volution car runs on air, the
23 company claimed that it caused low levels of pollution or no pollution at all.
24 However, some critics say that the car does contribute to pollution because the
25 electricity used to help power the car comes from fossil fuels. Regardless, these cars
26 would be better for the environment.

27   Another air-powered car, the LN2000, which is being developed at the University
28 of Wisconsin, is based upon the concept of the steam engine. The scientists involved
29 in these experiments decided to use nitrogen because it is so abundant because it

(continued on next page)

(continued from previous page)

> 30 makes up about 78 percent of the Earth's atmosphere. The liquid nitrogen used to
> 31 power this car is stored at –320 degrees Fahrenheit. The nitrogen is heated to a boil,
> 32 and then turns to gas just like boiling water turns into steam.
>
> 33   The LN2000 gives off very little pollution because releasing nitrogen back into the
> 34 atmosphere is relatively harmless. The LN2000 does produce the same type of
> 35 pollution as the e.Volution; electricity is used to power the car, and fossil fuels are
> 36 being used to create that electricity.
>
> 37   Right now, it may be difficult for you to envision your weekly commute without
> 38 the inevitable—and costly—visit to the gas pumps. However, in less time then you
> 39 can imagine, gasoline-powered vehicles will be a thing of the past. The influx of
> 40 SUVs and the abundance of drivers on the roads are detrimental to the environment.
> 41 It is time to consider a more realistic alternative.
>
> 42   Your Friend from the Future,
>
> 43   Alexis

1. What is the **best** way to change the sentence in lines 13–14 (*Consider the . . . Brignoles France.*)?

    a. Insert a comma after **Brignoles**.
    b. Insert a comma after **introduced**.
    c. Change *vehicle* to **vehikle**.
    d. Make no change.

2. Which transition would **best** fit at the beginning of the sentence in lines 34–36 (*The LN2000 . . . that electricity.*)?

    a. For example,
    b. Moreover,
    c. As a result,
    d. Nonetheless,

3. What is the **best** way to change the sentence in lines 16–17 (*Instead of . . . air pump!*)?

    a. Insert a comma after **Instead**.
    b. Change *most near* to **nearest**.
    c. Change the *exclamation point* to a **period**.
    d. Make no change.

4. The sentence in lines 24–25 (*However, some . . . fossil fuels.*) is poorly written. Which one of these is the **best** way to rewrite it?

   a. However, some critics say that's wrong. They say that the car does contribute to pollution. The electricity used to help power the car comes from fossil fuels.
   b. However, some critics disagree, stating that the electricity used to help power the car comes from fossil fuels.
   c. Because the electricity used to help power the car comes from fossil fuels, however, the car does contribute to pollution.
   d. If you want to listen to what the critics say, then you'll hear that this car and its electricity contribute to pollution.

5. What is the **best** way to change the phrase in line 42 (*Your Friend . . . the Future,*)?

   a. Change *Friend* to **Freind**.
   b. Change *from the* to **From The**.
   c. Change *Friend from the Future* to **friend from the future**.
   d. Make no change.

6. The sentence in lines 28–30 (*The scientists . . . Earth's atmosphere.*) is poorly written. Which one of these is the **best** way to rewrite it?

   a. The scientists involved in these experiments decided to use the abundant element nitrogen, which makes up about 78 percent of the Earth's atmosphere.
   b. The Earth's atmosphere, which makes up about 78 percent of all nitrogen, was used by scientists involved in these experiments.
   c. Nitrogen, the abundant element used by scientists involved in these experiments, was decided upon.
   d. Abundant nitrogens were used by scientists involved in these experiments, which makes up about 78 percent of the Earth's atmosphere.

7. What is the **best** way to change the sentence in lines 38–39 (*However, in . . . the past.*)?

   a. Change *will* to **would**.
   b. Remove the comma after **imagine**.
   c. Change *then* to **than**.
   d. Make no change.

8. Which of the following is the **best** way to combine the two sentences in lines 11–12 (*Alternative engines . . . of engines.*)?

   a. Alternative engines, electric, and fuel-cell-powered types of engines, power these vehicles.
   b. Alternative engines power these vehicles, including electric and fuel-cell-powered types of engines.
   c. Alternative engines vehicles, powered by electric engines and fuel-cell-powered engines, power these.
   d. Alternative engines, such as the electric and fuel-cell-powered types, power these vehicles.

9. Where is there an incomplete sentence?

   a. in line 10 (*One not . . . non-renewable resource.*)
   b. in lines 14–15 (*The exhaust . . . contain pollutants.*)
   c. in lines 22–23 (*Due to . . . at all.*)
   d. in line 41 (*It is . . . realistic alternative.*)

10. Which of the following is the **best** supporting detail to add after the sentence in lines 31–32 (*The nitrogen . . . into steam.*)?

    a. The Earth's atmosphere is about 21 percent oxygen.
    b. According to the researchers' estimates, a 60-gallon tank will allow the LN2000 to travel about 200 miles.
    c. The e.Volution originated in Europe, whereas this model, the LN2000, is an American-made car.
    d. You should be able to visit your local LN2000 dealership and pick one up today.

DELVING INTO THE EARTH

George's seventh-grade earth science teacher has asked each student to prepare a report about a location somewhere in the United States where a visitor could see examples of geological wonders. George recently took a trip with his family to New Mexico and toured the Carlsbad Caverns National Park. He wrote his rough draft about what he discovered on his trip. He needs your help editing and revising it.

Here is George's rough draft. Read it and then answer questions 1–10.

1 While traveling in the Southwestern United States, you may come across a
2 spectacular natural wonder: Carlsbad Caverns National Park. This park is a truley
3 magnificent example of the geological phenomena to be found in our country. It
4 boasts the largest single cavern in the world, the fifth-longest cave network in the
5 world, and the deepest cave in the United States.

6 The Kings Palace Tour will take you deep and far into the earth. The one-and-a-
7 half-hour ranger-guided tour took you almost a mile underground. A public tour will
8 take you about 830 feet below the surface. You can see columns, soda straws, and
9 draperies. If you decide to make this mighty trek, be sure to be in good health.
10 Children under the age of four are not allowed to make this difficult journey.

11 The Slaughter Canyon Cave Tour is a two-hour expedition through one and one-
12 fourth miles of underground passageways. There aren't any trails or electricity to
13 guide you on your way a ranger will be there to help you along anyway. All those
14 who go on this Tour will be equipped with a headlamp, however, from the Park
15 Service. This tour boasts some of the most fascinating columns in the world,
16 including the 89-foot-high Monarch Column and the Christmas Tree Column, which
17 is covered in semi-preshus crystals.

18 An experienced spelunker may want to try either the Spider Cave or Hall of the
19 White Giant Tours. Both last four hours and all participants are expected to be in
20 peak physical condition. You should also not have a fear of tight spaces or heights,
21 as tourists will crawl, climb, and squeeze their way through. This tour is not offered
22 to children less than twelve years of age.

23 Perhaps the most stunning activity open to visitors to Carlsbad Caverns is the
24 flight of the Mexican free-tailed bats. Each day at sunset in the summer, those bats
25 that dwell in the caverns from April to October will exit the cave in a
26 counterclockwise pattern. In August and September, the event is particularly
27 brilliant, as the young bats join their adult counterparts for the nightly flight.

28 Of course, not all of Carlsbad Cavern's activities require visitors to hike through
29 underground tunnels. In fact, there are many nature trails that wind their way
30 through the park's outdoor wilderness.

31 Touring Carlsbad Caverns is not for the timid or for the physically unfit. They
32 recommend that visitors be adequately prepared for all of their adventurous

(continued on next page)

(continued from previous page)

```
33  activities.  Do not mistakenly believe that the beauty of the landscape makes it any
34  less dangerous.  Dress appropriately, bring the right equipment, and have a good
35  understanding of what to expect in this desert area.  If you know what to expect and
36  have a taste for great adventure, then Carlsbad Caverns National Park is probably
37  the place for you!
```

1. What is the **best** way to change the sentence in lines 1–2 (*While traveling . . . National Park.*)?

    a. Change *traveling* to **travelling**.
    b. Change *wonder* to **wunder**.
    c. Change *Southwestern* to **southwestern**.
    d. Make no change.

2. George wants to add the following sentence to the fifth paragraph: *They perform the opposite feat at sunrise, returning to the cave before the sun can make its appearance in the sky overhead.* The sentence would **best** fit

    a. after the sentence in lines 23–24 (*Perhaps the . . . free-tailed bats.*).
    b. after the sentence in lines 24–26 (*Each day . . . counterclockwise pattern.*).
    c. after the sentence in lines 26–27 (*In August . . . nightly flight.*).
    d. before the sentence in lines 23–24 (*Perhaps the . . . free-tailed bats.*).

3. What is the **best** way to change the sentence in lines 15–17 (*This tour . . . semi-preshus crystals.*)?

    a. Change *boasts* to **boast**.
    b. Change *semi-preshus* to **semi-precious**.
    c. Change *world* to **World**.
    d. Make no change.

4. The sentence in lines 20–21 (*You should . . . way through.*) is poorly written. Which one of these is the **best** way to rewrite it?

    a. You should also not have a fear of tight spaces, heights should not scare you, as tourists will crawl, climb, and squeeze their way through.
    b. Tourists will crawl, climb, and squeeze their way through, so you should not have a fear of spaces or tight heights.
    c. Tight spaces or heights will scare you if you have a fear of them, so crawl, climb, and squeeze your way past the tourists.
    d. Also, a fear of tight spaces or heights will hinder you, since tourists are expected to crawl, climb, and squeeze their way through these caverns.

5. What is the **best** way to change the sentence in lines 13–15 (*All those . . . Park Service.*)?

   a. Change *Tour* to **tour**.
   b. Change *equipped* to **equiped**.
   c. Remove the comma after **headlamp**.
   d. Make no change.

6. Which of the following is the **best** supporting detail to add after the sentence in lines 29–30 (*In fact . . . outdoor wilderness.*)?

   a. The Old Guano Road Trail, a 3.7-mile above-ground path through a network of rock cairns, is a popular day hike.
   b. One of these tours boasts the 89-foot-high Monarch Column.
   c. Thank goodness you won't find yourself in the desert in the southwestern United States!
   d. Don't worry about bringing the proper equipment, however, since no visitors are expected to be prepared for the outdoors.

7. What is the **best** way to change the sentence in lines 6–7 (*The one-and-a-half-hour . . . mile underground.*)?

   a. Change *took* to **takes**.
   b. Insert a comma after **ranger-guided**.
   c. Change *to* to **too**.
   d. Make no change.

8. What is the **best** way to rewrite the sentence in lines 35–37 (*If you . . . for you!*) to improve the paragraph?

   a. Carlsbad Caverns National Park is probably the place for you! If you know what to expect and have a taste for adventure.
   b. Knowing what to expect and having a taste for adventure are just two reasons to come to Carlsbad Caverns National Park!
   c. If you're highly prepared and enthusiastic for outdoor adventures, then Carlsbad Caverns National Park is probably the place for you!
   d. Carlsbad Caverns National Park, if you know what to expect and have a taste for great adventure, is the place!

9. What is the **best** way to change the sentence in lines 2–3 (*This park . . . our country.*)?

   a. Insert a comma after **example**.
   b. Change *truley* to **truly**.
   c. Change *geological* to **Geological**.
   d. Make no change.

10. The sentence in lines 12–13 (*There aren't . . . along anyway.*) is poorly written. Which one of these is the **best** way to rewrite it?

    a. While trails, electricity, and rangers are not there, your way will help you along anyway.
    b. Trails and electricity there are not. On your way, a ranger will be there to help you along to guide you.
    c. Because trails and electricity are not there to guide the ranger on his or her way, no one is there to help you along.
    d. There are neither trails nor electricity to guide you on your way, but a ranger will be there to help you along.

ENHANCING REALITY

Isabella's seventh-grade industrial arts teacher has asked each student to write a report about a new kind of technology he or she hopes to see become part of normal everyday life within the next ten years. Isabella has visited the library, outlined her ideas, and written her rough draft. She needs your help editing and revising it.

Here is Isabella's rough draft. Read it and then answer questions 1–10.

1 Integrating video game technology into everyday life is one of the most innovative
2 ideas introduced in the past few decades. Augmented reality—the scope of which
3 includes pulling graphics typically only seen on television or computer screens and
4 mingling them with the real world—is by far one of the most advanced and thrilling
5 forms of technology being developed today. Imagine being able to enhance what we
6 see, hear, feel, and smell, all with the cooperation of modern video technology.

7 The concept of "virtual reality" has been around for quite a while now. This
8 graphic reality creates computer-generated environments and invites people into
9 them, allowing them to nearly become part of a video world. Augmented reality goes
10 a step further by adding graphics to and improving sounds and smells from the real
11 world. Just as many vehicles nowadays have Global Positioning Systems (GPS) to
12 help the driver plot directions and locate him- or herself on a map, people will be able
13 to get computerized information, about where they are and what they are seeing and
14 hearing. Simply by donning a pair of special spectacles, a person will have
15 information right before their very eyes—literally! The enhancements of sound and
16 sight will be refreshed every time the person moves his or her head.

17 Several high-tech companies and universities are exploring this new medium.
18 They hope to perfecting the means by which people can enhance what they are
19 having experienced in their environment. As with all scientific discoveries, however,
20 mistakes must be made in order to obtain the desired result.

21 A head-mounted display (HMD) resembles a pair of skiing goggles. It will allow
22 people to see graphics and text much like a computer monitor. Video see-through
23 displays block out the wearer's surroundings. They use tiny video cameras to
24 capture images of the environment. Like looking through the lens of a camera. The
25 person sees a video image of the real environment with graphics laid over that video.
26 Video see-through displays have one major problem: to much time lapses between
27 what the cameras capture and what they project to the person wearing the headset.

28 Tracking systems for augmented reality must be even accurater than those
29 systems currently in use, such as GPS. GPS can be as much as ten to thirty meters
30 off its target. A person using a similar device needs more precision than that. An
31 augmented reality system that projects images at a distance of twenty meters ahead
32 would be worthless to the person wearing it. Therefore, the tracking system must
33 still be refined in order for augmented reality to become part of our everyday lives.

(continued on next page)

(continued from previous page)

> 34   Technology has come far since Pong was first introduced to video arcades in the
> 35   1970s. Every year, we see video game graphics becoming smoother and more
> 36   advanced. Practical three-dimensional systems like augmented reality would
> 37   improve our lives considerably by making our knowledge of the world around we even
> 38   clearer. At the rate we're going now, within just a few years men and women from all
> 39   walks of life can experience augmented reality.

1. What is the **best** way to change the sentence in lines 14–15 (*Simply by . . . eyes—literally!*)?

    a. Change *have* to **has**.
    b. Remove the comma after **spectacles**.
    c. Change *their* to **his or her**.
    d. Make no change.

2. Isabella wants to add the following sentence to the third paragraph: *So far, the prototypes have been somewhat bulky and imperfect.* The sentence would **best** fit

    a. before the sentence in line 17 (*Several high-tech . . . new medium.*).
    b. after the sentence in line 17 (*Several high-tech . . . new medium.*).
    c. after the sentence in lines 18–19 (*They hope . . . their environment.*).
    d. after the sentence in lines 19–20 (*As with . . . desired result.*).

3. What is the **best** way to change the sentence in lines 26–27 (*Video see-through . . . the headset.*)?

    a. Change *to much* to **too much**.
    b. Change *they* to **he**.
    c. Insert a comma after **problem**.
    d. Make no change.

4. Where is there an incomplete sentence?

    a. in lines 5–6 (*Imagine being . . . video technology.*)
    b. in lines 38–39 (*At the . . . augmented reality.*)
    c. in line 7 (*The concept . . . while now.*)
    d. in line 24 (*Like looking . . . a camera.*)

5. What is the **best** way to change the sentence in lines 28–29 (*Tracking systems . . . as GPS.*)?

    a. Change *accurater* to **more accurate**.
    b. Change *than* to **then**.
    c. Change the *period* to a **question mark**.
    d. Make no change.

6. Which of the following is the **best** way to combine the two sentences in lines 29–30 (*GPS can . . . than that.*)?

    a. GPS can be as much as ten to thirty meters off its target, so a person using a similar device needs more precision than that.
    b. GPS can be as much as ten to thirty meters off its target, but a person needs a more precise device to rely upon.
    c. A person using a similar device, like GPS, needs more precision than that.
    d. As much as ten to thirty meters off its target, GPS is a much more precise device for people to use.

7. What is the **best** way to change the sentence in lines 11–14 (*Just as . . . and hearing.*)?

    a. Change *driver* to **Driver**.
    b. Remove the comma after **information**.
    c. Change *seeing and hearing* to **see and hear**.
    d. Make no change.

8. The sentence in lines 18–19 (*They hope . . . their environment.*) is poorly written. Which one of these is the **best** way to rewrite it?

    a. They hope that people can enhance what they are having experienced in their environment.
    b. In their environment, they hope to perfecting the way by which people can enhance their environment.
    c. By experiencing their environment enhanced, they hope to perfect the means by which people can enhance what they are having.
    d. They hope to perfect the means by which people can enhance their experiences of the environment.

9. What is the **best** way to change the sentence in lines 36–38 (*Practical three-dimensional . . . even clearer.*)?

    a. Change *clearer* to **more clear**.
    b. Change *improve* to **improved**.
    c. Change *we* to **us**.
    d. Make no change.

10. The sentence in lines 7–9 (*This graphic . . . video world.*) is poorly written. Which one of these is the **best** way to rewrite it?

    a. This graphic reality creates computer-generated environments. Invites people into them. Allowing them to nearly become part of a video world.
    b. By allowing them to nearly become part of a video world, this graphic reality creates computer-generated environments.
    c. This graphic reality, which creates computer-generated environments, invites people to almost become part of a video world.
    d. Creates computer-generated environments and this graphic reality invites people into them by allowing them to almost become part of a video world.

Thinking Ahead 54

Denver's history class has been studying Nostradamus, a man born in the sixteenth century whose predictions for the future of humankind have astounded historians and scientists alike for centuries. His teacher has asked each student to explain how Nostradamus was able to make predictions about a time so vastly different and distant from his own. Denver has devised his own set of ideas and written his rough draft. He needs your help editing and revising it.

Here is Denver's rough draft. Read it and then answer questions 1–10.

1 Consider the following true story: In 1898, Morgan Robertson published a novel,
2 *Futility*, in which a luxery liner called the *Titan* crashes into an iceberg one April
3 night while traveling through dense fog. In the story, the ship sinks and hundreds
4 of people die. Robertson claimed that the story came to him while he was in a trance.
5 Fourteen years following the book's publication, the *Titanic* fell to an identical fate,
6 which was similar in size and structure to the *Titan*. Even the reason for high
7 casualty numbers—too few lifeboats on board—was the same in both accounts.
8 Could Robertson have been unknowingly foretelling the future? Was it an
9 extrasensory experience or merely coinsidense?

10 People often claim that they have the ability to see into the future. In fact, some
11 people make a living off that claim. Is it truly possible to foretell what is going to
12 happen tomorrow or fifty years from now? Do certain people possess a sixth sense
13 called "extrasensory perception" (ESP,) which some believe to be beyond sight,
14 hearing, smell, touch, and taste? Many people are convinced that we all have the
15 ability to experience our world both physically and on some higher astral plane.
16 Others feel that only certain people can channel and harness this powerful energy.
17 The common belief among those who put faith in ESP is that some people are more
18 attuned to their perceptions than others.

19 By the common definition, ESP is not a bodily sense. Rather than being a
20 physical response to something in the environment, ESP typically manifests itself in
21 thoughts. There are several different kinds of ESP. Telepathy is the ability to read
22 someone else's thoughts. Clairvoyance is the ability to see something occurring in
23 another place. Precognition is the ability to see into the future.

24 The idea that people could perceive things outside of their bodily senses is not a
25 new one. However, ESP as we understand it does not develop until the twentieth
26 century. Duke University professor J.B. Rhine coined the term "ESP" in 1934. Rhine
27 was one of the first respected scientists to research and test paranormal phenomena
28 in a university laboratory.

29 Since it is exceedingly difficult to scientifically prove the existence of ESP, there
30 are many conflicting theories regarding how it works. Like religious concepts, ESP
31 does not fit into a scientific model. In fact, it similarly depends on the existence of a

(continued on next page)

(continued from previous page)

```
32  soul dwelling in a reality outside of the bounds of our physical laws. Some people
33  purport that ESP is a result of something coming from a place beyond the known
34  physical world. As time and space work differently in this parallel reality, believers
35  claim that people are allowed to easily flow in and out of other's thoughts and
36  sometimes can see the distant past and future. Our conscious mind may often be
37  unaware of this other plane, but phenomena will manifest still themselves from time
38  to time.

39      So was Robertson truly able to foretell the *Titanic* tragedy? Are the predictions of
40  Nostradamus mere coincidences? Or is it comforting for some people to believe that
41  we have a higher awareness of the world around us? It is hard to know for sure.
```

1. What is the **best** way to change the sentence in lines 34–36 (*As time . . . and future.*)?

   a. Change *parallel* to **parallell**.
   b. Change *other's* to **others'**.
   c. Remove the comma after **reality**.
   d. Make no change.

2. What is the **best** way to change the sentence in lines 1–3 (*In 1898 . . . dense fog.*)?

   a. Change *luxery* to **luxury**.
   b. Insert a comma after **iceberg**.
   c. Change *dense* to **dence**.
   d. Make no change.

3. What is the **best** way to change the sentence in line 39 (*So was . . .* Titanic *tragedy?*)?

   a. Change the *question mark* to an **exclamation point**.
   b. Change *foretell* to **fourtell**.
   c. Insert a comma after **Robertson**.
   d. Make no change.

4. Which of the following is the **best** closing sentence for the last paragraph?

   a. The best part of being an American is having the freedom to speak your mind.
   b. If you want to be a scientist, then I wouldn't suggest believing in ESP.
   c. Fortunately, it is the existence of mysteries such as this that make life more interesting.
   d. Whenever you come upon someone who appears to be a bit odd, you can safely assume that they are tapping into their subconscious mind.

5. What is the **best** way to change the sentence in lines 12–14 (*Do certain . . . and taste?*)?

   a. Remove the comma after **smell**.
   b. Change the *question mark* to a **period**.
   c. Change *(ESP,)* to **(ESP),**.
   d. Make no change.

6. Which transition would **best** fit at the beginning of the sentence in lines 6–7 (*Even the . . . both accounts.*)?

   a. However,
   b. Nevertheless,
   c. As a result,
   d. In fact,

7. What is the **best** way to change the sentence in lines 25–26 (*However, ESP . . . twentieth century.*)?

   a. Change *does* to **did**.
   b. Change *twentieth* to **twentyeth**.
   c. Remove the comma after **However**.
   d. Make no change.

8. What is the **best** way to change the sentence in lines 8–9 (*Was it . . . merely coinsidense?*)?

   a. Change *coinsidense* to **coincidence**.
   b. Change *it* to **he**.
   c. Insert a comma after **extrasensory**.
   d. Make no change.

9. Which of the following would be the **best** way to rewrite the sentence in line 16 (*Others feel . . . powerful energy.*) to make it more specific?

   a. Some people think that only certain people can channel and harness this powerful energy.
   b. Others feel that only certain people, such as psychics, shamans, or mediums, can channel and harness this powerful energy.
   c. Others feel that only others that they may or may not know can channel and harness this powerful energy.
   d. While others feel that only certain people can channel and harness this powerful energy.

10. The sentence in lines 5–6 (*Fourteen years . . . the* Titan.) is poorly written. Which one of these is the **best** way to rewrite it?

    a. After fourteen years, the book's publication about the *Titanic* showed a similarity between the fictional ship and its real-life size and structure, the *Titan*.
    b. The *Titanic* fell to an identical fate, which was similar in size and structure to the *Titan* fourteen years later.
    c. The book was published, the *Titanic* fell to an identical fate, the size and structure was similar, and the *Titan* came fourteen years earlier.
    d. Fourteen years following the book's publication, the *Titanic*, which was similar in size and structure to the *Titan*, fell to an identical fate.

Made in United States
Orlando, FL
14 February 2023